D1548332

Hacking Capitalism

Modeling, Humans, Computers, and Money.

Kris Nóva

Hacking Capitalism

Version 0.1.6

Modeling Humans, Computers, and Money.

978-1-68489-565-6

Edited by Ashley Bischoff

Table of Contents

Foreword

The 2021 United States Insurrection

January 6th, 2021

I had discovered four hits of San Francisco LSD a few hours before the insurrection began to unfold. The collision of these two events was seemingly coincidental.

I was watching live from the floor of my living room. I was living in Silicon Valley at the time. I was recovering from an eight-month-long bender of alcohol, a broken queer polyamorous relationship, and complete isolation because of the COVID-19 pandemic. I hadn't looked into the eyes of another human and smiled in months. My reality began to shift.

At this point, the absurdities of the tech industry and my unique experience as an openly transgender person were relatively insignificant compared to what was happening in my immediate world. Between the pandemic, the lockdown, the political hellscape that I found myself in, my unhealthy obsession with social media, and my addiction with alcohol, I had never been more broken or lost. "These people have no grasp on what reality they're actually living in." I thought to myself.

I also remember thinking to myself while snuggling my thirty-year-old stuffed tiger on the floor next to a pile of computer science textbooks, "Do I? Do I have any idea what reality I am actually living in?" Finally, the coup ended, and I turned off the television. The show was over, but my invasive thoughts about the U.S. persisted. That evening I hadn't been able to stop listening to Working Class Hero by John Lennon on repeat. There was a moment when I had considered that despite everything that had happened, this could've just been any other night in tech.

Sobriety

In 2021, I spent the entire year sober, coming to terms with my newly found awareness of this broken world that we're all living in. It had taken a year of clarity before the fog of my decade-long career to begin to lift. Throughout my tenure as an engineer, the three startups that I had worked at had seen (in total) over one billion dollars in acquisition payouts. But at the time, I was about three months away from spending the last of my payout savings on Grubhub, White Claw, and Costco vodka. I knew that I needed a new job, and I needed one soon.

I began interviewing again, and I soon received a substantial offer. At the time, I had outstanding offers from 5 of the 7 top profitable tech corporations in the U.S. I only needed to give up four years of my life, and a portion of the money would be mine. I made a decision, and I settled on a much smaller number for the next four years in exchange for cohesive transgender health coverage and the hopes of an inclusive working environment.

I had achieved a small amount of notoriety in my field, and I wasn't terribly concerned about finding employment. At the time of these interviews, I was unpredictably depressed and considering giving up on life. In one of the cases, an email from a prospective employer suggesting a quick Zoom call had been what swayed me from a bottle of narcotics. I was in rough shape, however I managed to survive.

The new job gave me the opportunity to have facial-feminization surgery, which has helped dramatically with my depression. After a few months of settling in to the new gig, I realized that I was looking at the world very differently. I was no longer in survival mode. I was finally able to achieve what I had set out to achieve. I wasn't totally sure when things had changed, but they did. It felt relatively free-I was no longer struggling to keep my head above water. The world seemed - calm - for the first time in my life. The more that I explored these thoughts, the more I realized that there was an enormous system that I had finally been able to break out of. That system is capitalism, and this book will help you understand how I hacked it.

Introduction

This book will teach you how to apply cybersecurity-exploitation modeling and tactics to help you thrive in your career in the tech industry.

What Will You Learn?

You'll learn how to influence the tech industry. You'll learn about the system's components, their relationships, and how you can influence their outcomes. You'll walk away with an understanding of the psychological and economic effects of the tech industry. The system is the tech industry. The tech industry is the system. And this book will teach you how to hack it.

Who Should Read This Book?

This book is for anyone who's interested in expanding their influence within the tech industry. This is not an average "how to start a tech career" book. This book is specifically designed to be a realistic, and often unattractive portrait of a life in tech. This book is for anyone who has (or will have) a relationship with the tech industry, with production systems, or with similar corporations and organizations. This book is for software engineers, devops engineers, security analysts, CEOs, VPs, directors, product specialists, marketing specialists, salespeople, and managers. And you don't need to know how to code to find value in this book.

The Hacker's Manual

You'll learn tactics modeled after cybersecurity and computer science. And you'll learn how to apply these tactics to the people, computers, and economy of the tech industry. This book is designed to offer marginalized technologists the vocabulary, a working model, and the tools and tactics to help them take advantage of an unbalanced and evasive system. This book draws inspiration from my professional history in Linux and Kubernetes security, distributed systems, kernel engineering, and cloud infrastructure. If you enjoy linear thinking, modeling complex relationships as systems, and learning the strategies that I developed to become a venture capitalist and senior principal engineer in Silicon Valley, then this book is for you.

What I hope for the book

The primary goal of this book is to offer an actionable guide for how you can break into the inner circles of power within the tech industry. It takes an enormous effort merely to exist as a worker within tech. So I want to let everyone know how they can occupy the top of the industry. My hope is that this knowledge will bring about greater innovation and healthier working environments for everyone. While it may not seem obvious, dismantling a system can be one of the most effective agents of change. This book will aid in dismantling broken economic systems of thought that can damage ambitious minorities trying to not only survive - but thrive in the industry.

Why I Wrote This Book

I wrote this book as a gift for my past self. Looking back on my career, I learned a lot of the lessons the hard way. If I could travel back in time, I'd walk up to the twenty-two-year-old version of myself, I'd quietly hand her this book, smile, and walk away. Because I've been very broken in my career, I want to arm the marginalized technologists of today with a weapon to combat toxic masculinity and cultural nationalism in the workplace. There's no reason that the next generation of underrepresented people in tech need to suffer as I did. I want to offer a comprehensive how-to guide that will give a competitive advantage to LGBTQIA+ people, people of color, and anyone who's about to get chewed up and spat out just because they aren't a privileged white man with a superiority complex. I also have hope that the privileged people at the top of the pecking order will read this book and have a small glimpse into the unreasonable amount of work, planning, and overachievement that's needed to even have a chance at competing with the higher class.

Setting Expectations

Not everyone will be able to do everything in this book. I can't do everything in this book. This book is designed to offer a set of principles and techniques that I've seen work well. I've been privileged to a lot of opportunities in my career. Not everyone will have that same experience or the same privileges that I've had. This book is designed to offer actionable constructs in many areas with the hope that a subset of the areas will help to increase the chances that less-privileged people will find success.

This book is designed to paint a picture of the absurd amount of extra effort required for less-privileged technologists to compete at the highest level in the tech industry. This book isn't trying to imply that someone needs to think, act, or do specific things to be successful in tech. It's possible to be successful in tech without going through the gauntlet of what this book suggests. There are thousands of jobs available for folks at any level to enter this industry.

Worker exploitation is a problem in the United States as well as in many other countries. The problem is getting worse with every generation. Understanding the system that is the tech industry will inevitably require a level of intimacy with the dangerous working conditions that are a consequence of worker exploitation. I can't stress enough the importance of protecting yourself from these conditions.

I also want to be clear that I'm not advocating for you to overwork yourself.

Explaining how a system works does not imply that I am advocating for its existence.

I am not suggesting that the system is logical or that the system is fair. I'm explaining how it works. This is a realistic depiction of the industry in all its toxicity. If you want to compete with the elite, this is how it's done. Do with this information what you will.

In short, this industry is heavily tarnished by ruthless

capitalism, a system which is repulsive, relentless, and unfair. Competing with the elite is extremely difficult. This book reflects these challenges.

Regardless of the state of the system, it's still a system. Humans can rationalize and conceptualize systems. Humans can exploit systems. Humans can model systems. Modeling the system and helping you to understand it is precisely what this book aims to do. You can then apply that knowledge to exploit the very system that exploits tech workers.

About You

This book needs to make a few assumptions about you, the reader, to be effective.

This Book Assumes That You're a Technologist-or That You Work in Tech

The book assumes that you're a technologist or a tech worker of some discipline, such as a software engineer, operations engineer, marketing specialist, director, product specialist, or similar. Regardless of your role, this book assumes that you're in the tech industry. In short, I assume that you're a tech worker. The book holds a vague definition of the term "worker" and a vague definition of "tech." If you feel like the tech sector is responsible for some or all of your existing or future paycheck, you fit.

This Book Assumes That This Is All New Information

The most outrageous assumption that this book makes is that the lessons and tactics covered here are new to you. So there's a chance that some topics that I cover will be ones that you're already well versed in. But to cover the information in the final chapters of the book, the foundation for that information needs to be well defined in the earlier chapters. The book and its topics, definitions, and lessons need to be internally scoped. The icons in the book will let you skip to specific chapters so that you can easily correlate topics to prior sections as needed.

This Book Assumes That You Have Explicit Goals within Tech

This book's next assumption is that you understand your goals. You should understand what you want the tech industry to provide to you. This is a particularly bold assumption because the vast majority of marginalized technologists (the people the book is structured toward) will have likely approached their career with a survivor mentality. In other words, the readers of the book likely haven't had the privilege of sitting down and daydreaming about what they hope that the tech industry will provide for them. The book will assume that you've spent some time thinking of very explicit goals with your approach to tech. Some examples of personal goals within tech:

- I'd like to double my salary within the next twelve months.
- I'd like to create a piece of technology and a reputation that I'm proud of, and I'll know it when I see it.
- I'd like become a VP of a publicly traded company within the next three years.
- I'd like to have a certain amount of money saved in the bank within the next two years.
- I'd like a job in tech to provide a certain amount of money for me to save.
- I'd like to learn how to become a staff engineer.
- I'd like to learn how to run a profitable business.

Not all goals will be achievable, and in many cases gender, skin color, religious background, or even mental disabilities can become obstacles that stand between a person and their goals. According to McKinsey analysis about 95% of VP-level positions are held by non-Black people. This book tries to be realistic about these inequalities while offering specific tactics and techniques to combat the inequalities. [1]

This Book Assumes That You Understand Some Computer-Science Basics

As you understand the lessons in the book, they'll be reinforced with supporting examples of how you can apply them in common situations.

The book assumes that you have the expertise of an entry-level or mid-level contributor in tech:

- You understand what a server is.
- You understand computing, networking, and storage as fundamental principles.
- You understand what a cloud provider does.
- You understand what it's like to work on an engineering team.
- You're familiar with some of the common points of contention within software engineering.

In other words, you should be familiar with the basics of what it takes to try to generate revenue with technology.

Marginalization

If you've been treated as insignificant, peripheral, or as an afterthought—or just flat-out disrespected—this book is for you. Throughout the book I'll refer to marginalization and to being underprivileged. It isn't my intention to take away anyone's truth or to claim that any lived experience is more valid than another. All marginalization is liable to be harmful. Some more than others. As far as this book is concerned if you feel marginalized, you are.

[1] https://www.mckinsey.com/featured-insights/diversity-and-inclusion/race-in-the-workplace-the-black-experience-in-the-us-private-sector

Reading the Book

This book will read like a novel, and it'll likewise serve as a reference.

- Keep the book on your desk as a reference.
- Read the book from cover to cover like a novel.

The book is structured like a textbook. And my personal experience is sprinkled within the pages. As you read the book, you'll notice that there are many icons within each section title. The icons serve as visual cues to help you correlate certain topics and terms throughout the book.

Annotations in the book

Notes

These are generic notes.

These are single sentences that appreciate a pen and highlighter taken directly to the pages.

> This is a note…

Hacks

Hacks get to the point and tell you what you need to know. No bullshit hot takes that probably deserve someone such as yourself to post them on Twitter.

> This is a hack…

Definition

This is a formal definition I will use within the book. These definitions are explicit in nature, and in many cases are of my own design.

This is a definition…

Supporting Examples

This book will use authentic no-bullshit problems to illustrate the topics and lessons. It can be impossible to get a promotion. Not everyone will be able to stand up for themselves. There will be unconscious bias. The system is fundamentally imbalanced, and it isn't fair. These examples reflect this. I've intended these examples to be realistic. If I did my job well as an author, these examples should be relevant to marginalized readers.

This is an example…

Warning

These are warnings. As points are made, there will inevitably be dangers. Consider these statements your warnings of danger.

This is a warning…

Applied Hacking

These sections will be specific content on how to apply a given lesson. In other words, these are the "Applied Hacking" sections.

Many chapters will include an Applied Hacking section immediately before the conclusion as a way of reinforcing the lessons of a given chapter.

Disclaimer

This book doesn't offer legal advice. This book doesn't suggest that any economic system is better than another. This book doesn't teach you how to break into computer systems. This book doesn't encourage any illegal actions.

Chapter 1. The System

The tech industry is a ruthless system. But the tech industry is predictable.

Like all systems, we observe inputs, outputs, constraints, consequences, relationships, and components. The tech industry is no different.

Within the tech industry, there are smaller psychological subsystems, economic subsystems, and technical subsystems. Each with its own behavior, resiliency, constraints, and impact. Some of these subsystems are chaotic, while some are profoundly stable.

The tech industry is the amalgamation of these subsystems into a broader industry. The industry exists because humans want to profit with computers. The subsystems exist as the implementation details that enable the broader system to function. Technology has no concept of profit. The empirical glue that binds the technology to the economy is the tech industry.

The Tech Industry is the collective mesh of humans trying to profit with computers.

More specifically, the tech industry is the hardware, software, corporations, foundations, organizations, and their humans. Discussing the system won't advocate for the system or its behavior. But I'll attempt to explain how the system works, how to break it, and how to influence its outcomes.

The system is composed of subsystems, components, and their relationships.

I, Kris Nóva, the author of the book, have a relationship with the tech industry. You, the reader of the book, also have a relationship with the tech industry if you don't already. We'll discuss these relationships. We'll also discuss the relationships between the tech industry's subsystems as well as their relationships to humans like you. My relationship with the tech industry is weathered. I was never given a proper introduction. My ability to model the tech industry in this way is a reflection of my frustration in this lack of technical introduction and systemic modeling.

The tech industry overall has changed my life for the better. But these changes haven't come without severe consequences of trauma, loss, and discomfort.

The tech industry, despite its flaws, has allowed me to dream bigger than I've ever thought possible. But this has come at a cost to myself. This cost can be represented as a zero-sum subsystem known as exploitation.

Exploitation

> **Exploitation** is the action or fact of treating someone unfairly in order to benefit from their work.

The book will use this term to mean literally as it is defined. Exploitation will imply a sense of unfairness, or inequality that exists between one entity and another.

> **Zero-sum Exploitation** is exploitation when the gain of one side is lost by, or taken from the other.

In other words, the spoils of the situation are taken from the losing entity.

Similar to the conservation of energy, resources cannot be created or destroyed. The resources must come from somewhere and can only be traded or exchanged. In exploitative working environments resources are taken, or harvested, from the workers.

This exchange of resources (or the taking of resources from workers) is often justified in the eyes of the tech industry.

Not all working environments will be as cutthroat and ruthless as this simplistic view of the working industry. To be clear, there are healthy working environments where there's great opportunity to work without risk of zero-sum exploitation. But the tendency of the system will be to drift away from nonexploitation.

I believe the most favorable of working conditions to be a group of motivated, well funded, and supported individuals who are given an opportunity to achieve more as a group than they would have been able to achieve in isolation.

Unfortunately, in my experience, these ideal conditions are rare.

The term exploitation often has a dark and malicious connotation. Despite this connotation, I'll at times attempt to brighten and romanticize the term. I put forward that exploitation is fundamental for the tech industry to function. I'll use the term in its most literal sense, and at times exploitation will be one of my deliberate goals. Where there's unfairness, there's opportunity to exploit or be exploited. I don't shy away from that.

The working economy that governs the planet is vast. The country specific economy is a smaller component of the vast global economy. The tech industry is a portion of these smaller economies. Regardless of how much of an impact the tech industry has on other larger economies one simple truth remains:

> Because the tech industry exists within Capitalism, the tech industry is built on various levels of exploitation.

Which implies the corporations that compose the tech industry will deliberately be harvesting workers for resources.

> Don't worship companies, folks.
>
> The happiest tech people I know are the ones that realize that tech companies are taking advantage of you, and you have to do everything you can to reclaim as much value as possible. [2]
>
> – Shantini Vyas, iOS Engineer at Twitter

Chances are you have been treated unfairly at some point in your life. In other words, there has likely been a situation where you have been the victim of zero-sum exploitation and somebody has benefited at your expense.

If you find yourself working as part of an underrepresented group in the tech industry this is inevitably a familiar feeling.

All jobs will require some amount of work. Obviously some more than others. All jobs within the tech industry, likewise will require some amount of work.

Eventually, somebody will benefit from this work. Where there is limited benefit, there will be competition. If you aren't competing, you are less likely to see the benefit from your work.

The inability to share the load and the benefits are a consequence of competition. In my experience these conditions are capable of exploiting you if you aren't proactive in first exploiting them. It is the system's nature to exploit something. I urge you not to let that something be you.

 There is only one winner in a zero-sum game.

The concept of one winner is, by definition, competitive. Competition can be dangerous, and it can harm others.

Understanding exploitation can help you understand how to take advantage of the tech industry, which can in turn offer insights into the thinking that has created the industry itself. This is possible while remaining kind, compassionate, direct, collaborative and ethical.

> Exploitative thinking can be dangerous, but that doesn't mean that you should also be dangerous. Be kind to one another out there. The tactics in these pages won't work without compassion for yourself and others.

You'll find a glaring example of how exploitation, competition, and a zero-sum mentality can harm people by examining the group of people currently sitting at the operator's bench of the tech industry.

The Elite

There will be an ever-present antagonist lurking at the top of the industry. I specifically reserve the word elite to refer only to this group of ruthlessly competitive people at the top. There's no firm criteria on what someone needs to have to be considered a part of this group. In my experience, the elite typically have some common characteristics. The elite are externally competitive and internally collaborative. The elite embrace capitalism and the constructs taught in this book.

> The elite are externally competitive.

This group values competition and competitive behavior. Particularly with anyone who doesn't look like them or complacently work under them. This group tends to associate vulnerability with weakness, and they associate this perceived weakness with risk. An upshot of this perception is their reluctance to relinquish decision-making power within an environment by allowing "outsiders" into their space. They tend to consider that to be a "positive" outcome from a financial perspective.

> The elite are internally collaborative.

Their desire to maintain decision-making control makes it safe to assume that the elite tend to band together. Introducing diversity and new ideology into the group is something that they perceive as a risk. A ramification of this is that the elite often look the same and think the same. It'll be very difficult getting yourself inserted into their circles if you don't look and act just like the rest of them.

> The elite embrace capitalism.

The elite understand capitalism, and so they understand that profit is the only goal of this industry. The elite consider the harmful and damaging consequences from their actions to be valid operating costs. "This is business" seems to be their way of rationalizing their immoral behavior. If you're a marginalized person, you should be prepared for their obsession with profit to cause catastrophic consequences in your career if it hasn't already. The elite will not only understand capitalism-they embrace it. Who exactly is in this group is up to each reader. My definition of elite might be different from yours. I might consider certain people that I encounter to be elite, and you might not. I'll let the elite groups that we observe at the top of the tech industry speak for themselves. We all know who they are.

> What's relevant is that you aren't a part of this group, but you want to engage at their level.

Redirection

As you understand how to unpack the tech industry, you'll need to consider your energy reserves. The ability to redirect energy can subsidize this need. The tech industry as a system is extremely powerful. With this power comes a tremendous impact and, in some situations, devastation.

> **Redirection** is pointing existing effort to a new or different place, or for a new or different purpose.

There will be many tactics ranging from simple self-care tips to complete paradigm shifts on how to manage ruthless profit motivated Capitalism. These tactics can be used to redirect the force of the tech industry as you see fit.

Redirection is a mental system that can be applied to many situations and environments within the tech industry. It is the technique of focusing harmful or destructive energy intended for yourself, towards something productive.

For example a leader at a tech company may decide that your presence is no longer valuable on a specific project. There may be a large amount of energy focused on removing you from the project. Redirection is the ability to re-target that energy towards something positive such as removing alternative parts of the project that have been counter-productive in the past.

The tactics described in the book will often times follow this pattern of redirection. In the same way that aiki a form of Japanese martial arts is the practice of redirecting an opponent's power against themselves, this book will enable you to lead and influence the power of the tech industry back on itself. [3]

This is a dramatic paradigm shift in rationalizing the industry. The more powerful the tech industry is, the more available resources you will have to leverage for your own incentive. In other words, the more intimidating the situation is the more energy you have to redirect in your favor.

> Learn to embrace redirection. The more powerful the assailant, the more energy can be redirected for your agenda.

System Overview

The tech industry has predictable behaviors. The industry becomes easier to predict as you learn to observe the smaller elements that make up the broader machinery. The ability to predict the system can be extremely useful if you can apply these predictions toward your personal goals. For instance, your personal goal might be to double your salary in the next twelve months.

The industry is built on competition, which implies that some workers are better suited for the job than others. Competition exists both in the markets, and in the very organizations, projects, and companies that compose the industry. There is a direct relationship between money, and the amount of competition in a given environment. The current position of yourself, a product, or an organization within competitive environments is liable to impact the amount of money that can be harvested in the environment. Especially if the environment is highly valued.

A desirable goal is to find environments with an inverse relationship between competition and value.

> In general, the less competition in a highly valued space, the better.

Your understanding of where the industry has an abundance of resources will also hint at where you can find these higher paying jobs. The ability to parse this information from the industry comes from an understanding of how the system works. The ability to do it well comes from understanding the system well.

This understanding can help you refine your search to find details that can promote your goals.

The Nature of The System

The tech industry cares about one outcome: **profit**.

The tech industry is ruthless in its hunt for profit. Much like a virus, the system seems to infect those who were previously hurt by it. As workers spend more time submersed in the system, the likelihood they will be abused by the system increases. And the system will attempt to annihilate anyone who stands in the way of the system itself and whatever it deems as profitable—even more so if they're a marginalized person. Furthermore the system of the tech industry is likely to be better funded, and resourced than any younger alternatives such as worker unions or salary transparency efforts.

The Predictability of The System

The system and its various subsystems and components have chaotic elements and predictable elements. By noticing the predictable elements and which relationships you can lean into, you'll be able to position yourself strategically. Subsystems and components have outcomes. Subsystems and components generate other components. Human behavior, computer science, and economic principles affect one another. By modeling these relationships, you can understand how to exchange one element for another.

The system is ruthless - but predictable. You can exploit predictable.

Occupancy of The System

If we understand that the nature of the system is to seek profit at all costs, we can attach ourselves to profit streams.

By attaching ourselves to profit, we can leverage the system for a more effective ride to the top. The tech industry is powerful, resourceful, and extremely efficient at its quest for profit. It will be difficult to fight the system, change it, or deter it from its course. However, it will be easy to leverage the system for whatever indicative and goals you might have.

Recursion within The System

From a macro perspective, you can usually explain why the system did what it did. You can almost certainly connect the observed behavior of the system to profit. But just because you can explain an observed behavior doesn't mean that you can always predict future behavior. The system will seem sporadic and chaotic at times. An understanding of the smaller components can offer insights into which direction the macro system may pivot next. Another way of framing this is to compare this behavior to recursion in computer science. Imagine a single macro system of the tech industry that's perhaps the size of Earth's economies. And within this macro system there are an infinite number of potential smaller systems. Each subsystem's surface area resembles bubbles. These subsystems contract, expand, and cycle back into themselves. These subsystems exchange their components with smaller or larger surface areas as they group together and break apart. Where there's a well established surface area, there will be an opportunity to predict the system. The tech industry is metaphorical profit-driven foam. Your opportunity will come in the form of finding the surface of a nearby bubble and riding it to the top.

> Look for stability and well-defined intellectual boundaries to predict the system and its subsystems.

Machinery

Each subsystem will have its own behavior and its own nature. Most of which will be equally profit motivated as the macro system. These subsystems can be found in the form of companies, organizations, projects, or corners of tech. The macro system and its subsystems are composed of the same basic components. These components come in the form of economic and organizational structures, psychological patterns, and a never-ending contrast of technical debt versus profits. These components and subsystems are what compose the machine, or system, of the tech industry. At times, we'll be discussing the parts of this machine. How to build the parts, how to break the parts, how be an effective machinist, and how to design efficient machinery. I'll first define these principles, and then I'll explore their relationships.

Components

Components are concepts that compose larger systems. Components may behave as a broader system or as a smaller subsystem—or it may simply exist as the static fabric that composes something larger. These are specific patterns that can be observed, and in many cases they're predictable.

> **A component** is an element of a larger system; a concept.

When a component is in action and there's a clear outcome, you call it a subsystem.

A subsystem is a component of a larger system with a clear cause and effect; inputs and outputs.

In other words, systems are made up of components. Components that can be observed with clear cause and effect can also be referred to as subsystems. The exact labels and constraints of the paradigm aren't important. What is important is that you begin to think about composing larger systems of smaller systems, while imagining the impact and relationship the pieces have with each other.

Behavioral Components

There are two main behavioral components that deeply influence patterns in the tech industry. Specifically, these two components will help you understand the nature of a corporation in tech.

- Competition
- Collaboration

These two components are antisystems of each other. These will be fraught with conflict. This conflict is expected, and it can be predicted.

Psychological Components

There are also two main psychological components. These are states of mind that we can find scattered throughout the industry. Each is necessary for the industry to exist.

- Building
- Breaking

These two components are also antisystems of each other. There will be many opportunities in the tech industry to build outstanding monuments of achievement. Likewise, there will be many opportunities to destroy these monuments. It's likely that a single effort will never be completed before something attempts to destroy it. Like the conflict between competition and collaboration, this too can be predicted.

Technical Components

There are two technical components that are just as relevant in computer science as they are in exploiting the tech industry. These two concepts are classic examples of antisystems in my mind.

- Simplicity
- Complexity

In computer science, you can often exchange simplicity for flexibility. The trade-off is complexity. Complexity is difficult to maintain, but it can be worth the maintenance burden at times. Simplicity is easier to maintain, but it can be limited in what it can offer. These two concepts illustrate perhaps more than any other the relationship of antisystems. An understanding of the components can be used to predict their outcomes, which will in turn let you predict broader systems. We want to be able to clearly see that these patterns recursively repeat themselves on larger and smaller scales throughout the industry. As you understand the components, you may find yourself asking a few fundamental questions.

- What do I do with this new knowledge?
- How do I leverage this knowledge?
- What rules do I follow while managing this knowledge?
- What mindset do I carry with me as I navigate this knowledge?

Relationships

We also need to discuss how the tech industry's relationships change over time and how they respond to various inputs. Similar to how calculus can model equations, we'll need to model components of the tech industry in the same way. In other words, we'll need language that can explain how various constructs can interact with one another in the industry. This language can be useful to discuss the relationships independently of the components themselves. There will be moments in the book where we'll discuss abstract concepts such as changing or influencing your relationship with a component. Having an understanding of the terms used to discuss the relationships cemented will let you dig into greater detail later. Here are basic, common patterns that you'll find throughout the book.

Direct relationships

When one component of a system increases in response to another component increasing is what scientists would refer to as a direct relationship. A simple example of a direct relationship is the correlation between influence and income.

> As your influence goes up, so can your income.

Your ability to influence an organization in tech can have a direct impact on the amount of money you earn. There's an entire chapter on influence later in the book that will explain exactly how to grow your influence.

Inverse Relationships

You might also observe what scientists would refer to as an inverse relationship. This relationship is the inverse of direct relationships. As one component increases, the other decreases. You can find a simple example of this type of relationship in software systems. Particularly when it comes to showing options to a user. If you want a more simplistic system, you reduce the number of options that you show to the user. As the number of options goes down, the simplicity of the system goes up.

> As the number of options goes down, the simplicity of the system goes up.

Opposite and Opposed

The exact same system can be cast in many ways. Including its opposite and opposing components. Here is the same inverse relationship mentioned above, but it's now cast differently.

> As the number of options goes up, so does the complexity.

You can also flip the wording from "complexity" to "simplicity" to create the same relationship as its inverse.

> As the number of options goes up, the simplicity goes down.

The same relationship can be understood in many ways, and it can often be simplified. In other words, every inverse relationship can be simplified to a direct relationship simply by changing the wording.

This is important as this lets you call out trends in the tech industry that might not otherwise seem correlated. This also lets you connect correlating systems together to understand more complicated machinery.

Direct Relationship	More of This	More of That
Inverse Relationship	More of This	Less of That
Opposite Relationship	Less of This	More of That
Opposed Relationship	More of This	More of non-that

These relationships will not always be called out explicitly. I advise you to learn to identify them both in this book, and in your own experience in the industry. The ability to identify them will be critical as you will be able to use the relationships to model how to address your needs and goals.

For example if you are able to identify that you need more support in your project, and you also have noted that meeting deadlines has a direct relationship to support. You can conclude that meeting deadlines will provide support your project.

Linking Systems

You can link outcomes of previous systems to other systems. These links can be represented by the different relationships. For example, since you can correlate influence to income, you can also correlate income to impact. So you can draw a fairly reliable conclusion that an effective way to increase your impact in the tech industry is to increase your influence. In other words, if you have a goal to disrupt the tech industry, one way to increase your likelihood of success would be to increase your influence.

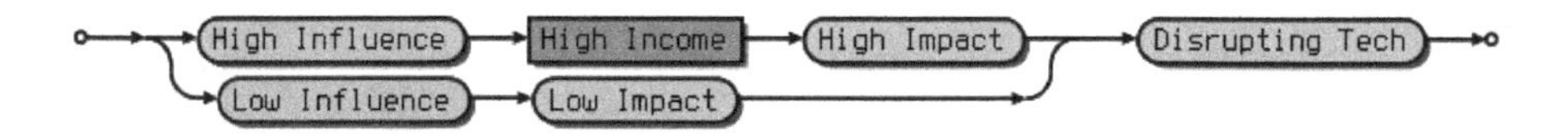

This workings of the tech industry isn't necessarily guaranteed, and it likely becomes less reliable with every connection. But the basic mechanics and trends are important to understand. You might not ever be able to guarantee that a system will work exactly as predicted. But you can try your best to structure your presence in the tech industry as strategically as possible while keeping these trends in mind.

In other words, there are trends but there are no guarantees. This is especially true for minorities and marginalized technologists.

Resources

Systems trade resources for products, typically in conjunction with unwanted byproducts.

> A **Resource** is a raw material, money, staff, time, or other supporting asset which can enable operation

Resources can be anything including human being or build pipelines. The tech industry will typically interact with resources related to people or money. Technology will typically view resources as raw materials, specific technologies, products, or methodologies. Resources are what fuels, or powers the various systems.

The ability to find these resources, and the wisdom to do so to empower one's own initiatives is known as being resourceful.

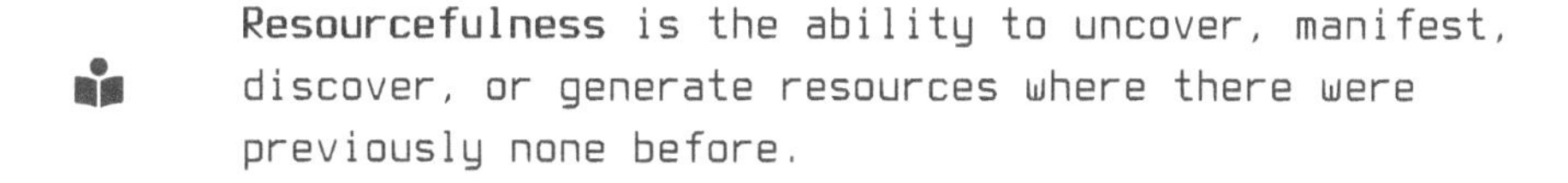

Resourcefulness is the ability to uncover, manifest, discover, or generate resources where there were previously none before.

Resources are a fundamental part of sustaining the tech industry. Without resources, the tech industry would have nothing to consume. In the same way that many engines consumes gas as a resource, the machine of the tech industry consumes workers as a resource.

Antisystems

These relationships will be important to unpack in order to see the internals of the broader tech industry.

There will be a specific relationship that we will need to understand before we can enumerate the basic components of tech. This relationship is found throughout the industry, and has special characteristics. The relationships will be referred to as antisystems.

An **antisystem** is an antithetical yet necessary counterpart to an existing system.

A system and its antisystem combined create broader, predictable systems with fascinating behavior.

This book introduces a new term to describe complimentary yet opposing binary systems. We first understand a system, then we understand it's opposing and necessary partner to be it's **antisystem**. These two systems exist in a mutual dichotomy, yet are necessary for either to exist.

There are many examples of antisystems in the natural universe. The concept of "chaos" and it's companion "order" seem to be as reciprocal as day and night while also conflicting in their nature. Binary star systems behave like atoms in a molecule, while opposing each other they also are the forces that create the broader structure. Without their attracting and opposing forces, the broader structure would fail to exist. Without chaos, there would be no order. Without a system, there would be no antisystem. There will be many examples of antisystems called out in the book.

Antisystems will help us understand where we can expect patterns in tech to repeat themselves. Antisystems will also intrinsically be surrounded with conflict.

Hacking

> **Hacking** is an attempt to exploit or gain unauthorized access of a system.

Hackers don't wait for doors to open. They find them and open them. Hackers ask for forgiveness instead of permission. Hackers are creative and resourceful.

These characteristics can be very effective at succeeding in business. I often say that the only difference between a hacker and successful entrepreneur is that the entrepreneur picked a legal target to exploit. There are many valuable characteristics that hackers and successful industrialist have in common. Perhaps their most important skill is a hacker's ability to observe the state of the world and find spaces for opportunity. The likelihood that a wide-open door will present itself is rare. But it's much more probable that a small overlooked detail will lead to another overlooked detail. That can lead to an opportunity that can bypass an otherwise blocked course.

Attention to Detail

If you're like me, and you find yourself in an underrepresented group in tech, you'll need to find ways to elevate yourself to compete with the elite. Attention to detail can be an effective way to bring yourself up to speed with others in the industry. Where there's attention to detail, there's a higher probability of finding an overlooked opportunity. You can exchange time and patience for a higher probability of success.

Read the fine print.

Where there's space for interpretation, there's space for misuse. This is a rule of thumb that's often used maliciously, but it still remains effective when applied productively. One example that we can borrow from is from the open-source software ecosystem. This example demonstrates that a goal-oriented mindset can predict a system's behavior. By predicting the behavior, the hackers harvested it as resource. We want to do this with tech-except ethically.

In 2020 a group of well-known online build services let you run arbitrary workloads for continuous delivery pipelines for free. A group of malicious users were able to masquerade as common open-source projects and use these services as unpaid computing resources. Naturally, these free and readily available computing resources were applied toward crypto mining.

So the malicious users were able to execute these workloads within the constraints of the tools while blatantly misusing them for their own profit. This example is unethical, and it shouldn't be recreated. But the mindset remains valuable to explore. The hackers saw the resources as opportunity, and they exploited this opportunity. You can learn from this and adjust the intent behind it to align with your goals. You can reposition your goals from an otherwise harmful tactic to one that you can use productively.

Be resourceful.

Tactics can be used for good or evil. The hackers knew what they wanted, and they took advantage of this opportunity. This mindset is exactly the mindset that you want to borrow from. You can use this mindset to your advantage. You can use this mindset to leverage the industry in your favor. The value is your ability to be resourceful.

Conclusion

The tech industry is a ruthless and predictable system made up of components, subsystems, relationships, and people.

The tech industry exists as a subsystem inside a broader capitalistic economy. Because the tech industry exists within capitalism, the tech industry is anchored to the nature of capitalism.

Thus, **profit** will always serve as the one and only goal of the system.

Learning to truly understand the nature of this system is helpful. But learning how to translate the nature of this system into your waking life with specific names and faces that you see every day is much more difficult. There are many techniques, such as redirection, that can serve as effective tools in helping to position the forces of the tech industry in your favor. Learning to wield these tools effectively is critical to influencing, and disrupting the tech industry.

Exploitation is a very real attribute of life within the tech industry. As a leader you will need to be aware of your exploitative nature. As a worker you will need to be weary of being over exploited. Each day that you're working in tech you're susceptible to being either directly exploited or exploited by proxy. Each day is an opportunity for you to understand the rules of the game and ward off the exploitation using as many tactics and techniques as you can gather.

There will be more techniques than those found in this book. Similar to learning Linux or a text editor, you will be privileged to a lifetime of learning and collecting tips, tricks, and techniques.

If you currently have a relationship with the tech industry, the clock has already started. Somebody, or something, will likely already be working towards profit.

The quest for profit can come with your support rallying behind it or at your expense. Be aware that being deliberate about your relationship with profit will be required to prevent exploitation.

Exploit the system before the system exploits you.

In my opinion without a deliberate plan, somebody or something will always be exploited in the zero-sum game of life within tech.

[2] @Shantini, Twitter, https://twitter.com/*shantini*/status/1467535174619787265

[3] Aiki, Martial Arts Principle, https://en.wikipedia.org/wiki/Aiki_(martial_arts_principle)

⚖ Chapter 2. Competition

The concept of competition dominates the tech industry, and it explains the behavior of the industry. Understanding exactly how competition affects the tech industry and where it comes from will let you predict the tech industry's subsystems, and it can help to protect you from harm.

Competition is the process of working in rivalry with the intent of outperforming others working towards the same goal.

You'll be competing in the tech industry, whether you would like it or not. You might not be deliberately competing with others or even realize that a competition is occurring - but they'll certainly be competing with you. Additionally, competition will happen at multiple levels within the tech industry.

- You'll be competing with other technologists for jobs.
- You'll be competing with your peers.
- Companies will be competing with one another.
- In large companies, business units can end up competing with one another.
- Even teams and engineers can end up as competitive rivals.

If you work at a tech company, there are likely internal channels specifically dedicated to your competition. Most companies will have dedicated Slack channels, email lists, and special-interest groups dedicated to watching and discussing known competitors in the industry. And as a technologist grows closer to the elite in title or influence, their ability to recognize this competition tends to heighten.

It's no secret that competition is relevant to the tech industry. But it took a global pandemic, some good LSD, and some of my own ingenuity for me to couple the behavior that I was experiencing every day back to the economy.

This link between the economy and competition in tech comes to mind whenever I think of my time in Silicon Valley in 2020. When I think of Silicon Valley, I think of the consequences of capitalism, such as the overexerting, stoic, of competitive personalities.

Personally, competitive personalities have hurt me, deeply. I remain hyper vigilant after identifying a noticeably competitive individual in the wild.

> The tech industry was forged in Capitalism, thus the tech industry is bound by competition.

The tech industry was born into competition because the tech industry was born under capitalism. Understanding capitalism is going to be critical in understanding how you can take advantage of the tech industry and why the tech industry is polluted with competitive personalities.

Capitalism and Free Enterprise

The consequences of capitalism are extremely visible and unfortunately extremely disruptive to the daily lives of anyone in the tech industry.

There are positive and negative effects of capitalism.

Capitalism can be used in productive ways, and capitalism can also be used in very selfish and harmful ways.

Capitalism is one of many types of economic systems. The United States practices an economic system that's closely aligned with profit-motivated capitalism with private and free markets.

After a short economics overview, I'll correlate capitalism with the tech industry by examining the consequences that you can observe in the tech industry.

These short economic lessons will be important in understanding competition.

Capitalism is an economic and political system in which a country's trade and industry are controlled by private owners for profit, rather than by the state.

As you grow in title and influence within a company or organization, you'll inevitably grow closer to the capital. So capital's impact and influence will become more relevant. This visibility and relevance of capital is an often-missed nuance within the tech industry.

So I've decided to give it a formal term.

Closer to the Market is a term used to illustrate that as an individual grows in title and influence the impact and influence of the competitive market economy will become more relevant.

For example a VP of a publicly traded company might be *closer to the market* than an individual contributor as the responsibilities of a VP will often involve managing revenue streams and some instance of a market or profit strategy.

The elite are also *closer to the market*.

Because of this relationship to competitive markets, the elite concern themselves with the quest for profit every moment of every day.

If you plan on communicating with them, you're going to have to speak their language. I suggest becoming as fluent as possible in the mechanics of business by researching state of the art business strategy and educating yourself on the mechanics of capitalistic business. Specifically startup and growth culture in the tech sector.

In the same way that you have a relationship with various technologies, you'll inevitably need to develop a relationship with business, competitive markets, and ultimately the economy in its entirety.

> You'll need to develop a relationship with capitalism.

Developing a deep understanding of business from an economic and profit perspective can offer tremendous insights into the motivation and behavior of the elite. The most telling aspect of the capitalist economic system is the competition between private owners. Capitalism is fueled by competition, and the players in the game are private owners.

Private Owners

It's safe to say that most companies are corporations. The ones that matter in the tech industry certainly are. All corporations in the United States, other than corporations that are structured as worker cooperatives [4] and the like, are controlled by private owners. These private owners control the means of production. There are similar paradigms in most other capitalistic countries.

> **Private Ownership** is the fact of being owned by a private individual, group, corporation, or organization rather than by a state or publicly governed body.

Private ownership, in this case, means that the corporation is operated without government intervention—or at least it's supposed to. These private (or non-government-controlled) corporations can be publicly or privately traded.

In other words, the government tends to stay out of the way of businesses. Which means that businesses in the tech industry have relatively free rein to operate as they see fit. This seems great in the eyes of the those who profit from the industry, but for an average tech worker, this can have extensively damaging consequences.

Businesses can be public (typically large and profitable) or private (typically young and in debt).

As you grow closer to the market, this concept of private ownership will become more relevant because the decisions being made often have to weigh human experience versus profit. This lesson will become particularly clear when I discuss ethics and more importantly the obligation—or lack thereof—for societal ethics.

The government, by design, stays out of the way of private owners unless they bring harm to the public at large (such as if a business were to pollute/damage the environment or the like).

Regardless of the semantics, the economic paradigm is straightforward. Which makes the behavior of the elite very predictable.

All corporations within the US exist under capitalism, and so in all likelihood, their private owners only care about one thing: **profit**.

Profit

The profit system is a simple system, with a single goal: earn more of it.

> **Profit** is a financial surplus; a financial gain after expenses

There are complexities with profit. Making a profit isn't always what it seems. It's possible for a person or group of people to make large amounts of money for themselves while a company remains unprofitable. It's also possible for a company to make a profit while its employees remain in residual debt.

> I like to compare profit at a company to water in a vessel. The money is the water. The company is the vessel.

This analogy illustrates the concepts of revenue, expenses, profits, and losses. Water is money, and the vessel is a bank account.

Revenue	Water flowing into the vessel
Expense	Water flowing out of the vessel
Profit	The water is rising
Loss	The water is draining

The vessel of water has a hole in the bottom, but there's a stream of water flowing into the top. As long as the vessel is taking on more water than it's losing, the vessel remains full. And whenever the water in the vessel rises, the vessel has made a profit. There are of course more complexities to the system as you explore deeper. Inflation, taxes, operating costs, operational runway, and so on. But the basic mechanics of the profit system really are that straightforward. Capitalism says every company must either make profit or at least come out even (such as with some charities and nonprofits). So every company tries as hard as possible to do so.

Increasing Profit

In the most basic sense, there are two ways to increase profit.

1. Increase revenue (*collect more water*)
2. Decrease expenses (*stop losing water*)

That's it. That's the entire model for how the elite frame every conversation. The system is simple. The system is elegant. The system is powerful. To be honest, I wish that more software engineers would build systems as simple as the profit system.

There are many strategies that try to focus on these two attributes. Some are complex, while some are simple. Perhaps the most basic way of conceptualizing this economic system is to look at the obvious paths to success.

The simplest way to increase revenue is to outperform your competitors.

The simplest way to decrease expenses is to extract more value from workers than they cost the company to employ.

Earlier I mentioned that capitalism is founded on worker exploitation.

> The tech industry often times can be, quite literally, technical-worker exploitation as a service.

In my opinion, the world is not always as cut and dry as these models present the information. Each situation is unique.

Within the study of economics we often acknowledge that an instance of an economy is never perfect. Instead of assuming an economy is perfect we address realism within our observations by identifying a perfect definition of something and measuring how far from perfect our observations are.

The same is true for worker exploitation, profit, and cutthroat capitalism.

Often times the situation is far from a totalitarian labor class, however measuring the distance from the edge can be helpful in modeling the situation.

The Henchmen

Understanding the system of profit and its relevance on capitalism can offer insights into how you can exist within a corporation in a capitalist economy. Particularly how the quest for profit can reward competitive behavior.

Tech is obsessed with finding ways of outperforming competitors because tech is obsessed with profit.

There is a group of profit-motivated people who are groomed specifically for this competitive environment. The group has little operational overhead, and they fit in nicely into the position of profit-motivated competition. The group behaves almost as if they were brought up or raised specifically to be prolific in this role.

The Henchmen are the group of aggressively competitive and low-overhead followers of the elite.

Henchmen (or perhaps more correctly Henchpeople) are easily motivated by profit. Capitalism rewards the henchpeople for doing what comes naturally to them: aggressively competing.

If a company values profits above all else, you can begin to understand why they might employ a small army of diabolical henchpeople. Especially if the company has every intent on increasing revenue by outperforming competition. The more competitive the henchpeople, the higher the likelihood that the company can turn a profit. The more aggressive these henchpeople are, the faster the company can turn a profit.

Their aggression and ambition can't be turned off. This suggests that their behavior is externally motivated because they do what they do even while straining others internally at a corporation. The henchpeople probably can't tell when competition is effective.

The henchpeople will likely try to compete with you.

I find the connection between ruthlessly competitive behavior and success within tech to be fascinating. This link is becomes more obvious once you begin paying attention to it.

In my experience there will be a comfortable landing pad for aggressive and stoic personalities at any tech company. These personalities fit in nicely, and they have very little trouble finding a home in the industry. Because of their competitive nature, they likely are directly relevant to profits or at least the notion to ruthlessly prioritize work in the hopes of making more money will come natural to them.

Additionally, henchpeople likely have experience advocating for themselves in times of conflict due to their competitive upbringing. This notion can be advantageous in competitive environments.

> Where there's profit, there will be henchpeople.

The henchpeople work on behalf of the elite, and most of the henchpeople don't even realize that they're a part of the group. In many cases, members of the henchpeople are promoted to the elite.

Masculine Socialization

In my opinion, masculine socialization directly leads to the ruthlessly competitive personality types that are rewarded within tech. This opinion is based on my experience as both a man and woman working in the tech industry.

> **Masculine socialization** is a set of ideals that start a young age and defines ideal (or perfect) masculinity as related to toughness, stoicism, heterosexism, self-sufficient attitudes, and a lack of emotional sensitivity. [5]

My prediction is that most men will have skipped this section, or will at least be "glossing over" these specific sentences.

If the ideals of masculine socialization are accurate, there's a likelihood that most men who meet these societal ideals will have viewed this correlation between competitive personalities and success in tech as an obvious antidote that isn't worth their time to learn or even acknowledge.

There is an interesting psychological effect that often occurs when seeking validation for these types of situations known as a **confirmation bias**.

> **Confirmation Bias** is the tendency to search for, interpret, favor, and recall information in a way that confirms or supports one's prior beliefs or values.

[6]

Essentially it can be common for individuals to find evidence for whatever it is they believe to be true. Regardless of their position on a topic, there will be ample evidence to support their belief.

In my experience, confirmation bias is common among ruthlessly competitive personality types. They see the evidence they need to flag something or someone as a risk, and block it out completely.

While most marginalized readers will find this information new and alarming, it will most likely bore most men as they view this to be well understood knowledge.

Reward

Capitalism seems to reward or favor ruthlessly competitive people who were socialized accordingly.

Capitalism works against everyone else, while effectively favoring narcissism and birth privilege.

As a transgender woman, it's hard for me to broach these topics without the construct of gender polluting my language. It's important in the context of the book to call out some general trends and some common outcomes of these trends. Understanding these trends can offer unique insights into why so many companies in tech look and behave the way they do.

According to Alessandra Cassara and Mary L. Rigdonc at the Department of Economics, University of San Francisco, San Francisco, CA "women enter competitions at the same rate as men when the incentive for winning includes the option to share part of the rewards with the losers (i.e., when the incentive system is socially oriented)" [7] which is a fascinating conclusion.

Women seem to favor altruism, which is evidently rewarded less in capitalism than self-interest.

In other words women seem to perform and receive less reward than men in competitive environments. Standford University has documented that women often respond less favorably to competition than men [8].

My personal experience as someone who has experienced adulthood in both masculine and feminine societal norms supports the idea that women often respond less favorably to competition than men. There are a lot of intangible personal circumstances that make male socialization what it is.

If we can draw any conclusions from the consequences of male socialization in the United States, perhaps the most obvious place to see the competitive trend is in men's paternity leave. A reluctance for men to take time away from the office, and society to begrudgingly offer maternity leave for women indicates a trend of society unfairly punishing women.

Here we find the current state of the tech industry: An industry born into capitalism, structured toward favoring competition. I've also seen a clear trend of society expecting men to exhibit competitive stoicism. Seeing an abundance of fiercely competitive men holding positions of power within the tech industry wouldn't come as a great surprise to me.

Capitalism rewards competition. Competitive personalities are bolstered by male socialization.

Where I find guarded positions of power in tech, I expect to find a surplus of competitive men.

Capitalism is built on the assumption that everyone who participates will have to focus on their own self-interest. A system that's structured on profit doesn't offer many incentives for generosity or kindness. Male socialization, especially in the United States, seems to be hyperfocused on self-reliant men who can provide for a family. There's no surprise that we also observe a trend of self-absorbed and narcissistic men who frame their view of the workplace around their ability to provide for themselves within it.

Regardless of how anyone was socialized, there will be an omnipresent undertone in tech of self-interest. You can expect to see quite a lot of it if you spend time in the tech industry.

Self-Interest

The concept of self-interest is what capitalism is built on. More specifically, it's the notion that you as a participant in the system are responsible for looking out for your own self-interest.

In my opinion anyone born into a country such as the United States is coerced into the economy, and not opting into the situation. Learning that self-interest is the default expectation can be a hard lesson to learn if someone finds themselves naturally caring, thoughtful, or altruistic in their nature.

> **Self-interest** is pursuing one's personal interest without regard for others.

The elite will almost exclusively focus on what they perceive as their own self-interest. And they'll have little practice auditing themselves and vetting their assumptions for what's in their best self-interest. The moment that you can influence what they perceive to be in their self-interest is the moment that you can influence their actions. This is exceedingly exciting, as their beliefs will be intrinsically hard to change afterward.

Implications of dark manipulation aside, this is a useful tactic for any underrepresented technologist.

The simple truth is that almost everyone in tech will have multitudes of lived experience with self-interest. Also, be prepared for different levels of comfort with how much control they may be willing to relinquish in exchange for a gamble on self-interest.

I often look at self-interest as a counterpart to competition. You can't have one without the other. Where there's competition, there will be self-interest. Where there's self-interest, there will be competition.

Selfishness and Selflessness

Three subtly unique topics are worth exploring when it comes to framing how you're going to fit into this competitive environment known as the tech industry. These topics focus on your relationship with yourself and how that relationship affects your relationship with others.

- Selfishness
- Selflessness
- Self-care

As you navigate the tech industry, you'll inevitably feel tension between selfishness and self-care. Having solid definitions for these words is important.

> **Selfishness** is lacking consideration of others; concerned primarily with one's own personal profit or interest; narcissistic.

Notice the subtle difference between my first definition and the next one. Selfishness comes at the expense of others. Self-care is focused primarily on yourself, without regard for others.

> **Self-care** is taking action to preserve ones own health or well-being.

Finally, selflessness is effectively the opposite of selfishness. It is focused primarily externally, with a disregard for yourself.

> **Selflessness** is concerned primarily with the needs of others than with one's own self; unselfish.

Take some time now and commit to memory that these terms have different meanings. I suggest holding these three terms in mind and looking up from the book for just a moment. With the terms in mind, look around and make a memory of the moment now that you can think back on later.

As I model the different terms, pay attention to the way that they affect others. It's possible to prioritize your own self-interest without causing harm to others.

Term	Self-interest	Impact to Others
Selfishness	✔	⬇
Selflessness	✖	⬆
Self-care	✔	⃠

Understanding the impact to others can explain why some organizations seem to feel more functional or dysfunctional than others.

Organizational Dysfunction

> **Organizational Dysfunction** is the counterproductive structure or experience that undermine the health, solidarity, and worth of an organization

Organizations within a company exist as a way of managing costs. Companies allocate a subset of their total resources to an organization and measure the results. This means that organizations have goals and limited resources. When accomplishing goals yields more resources for someone, that creates a naturally competitive environment.

Where there are limited resources, there will be competition for those resources.

> Despite sharing a common goal, competition may exist within an organization. This competition can lead to organizational dysfunction.

Competition may arise at any level within a company.

The layers of competition seem to come about somewhat chaotically. Employees might compete for pay but not for credit. One employee might compete with another for domain-knowledge expertise but not for applying any of the knowledge. In other words, the publication might be more important than the implementation. The credit may be more important than the execution. The VP may be rewarded for the work of her team.

And competition can shift with a single conversation. On Monday morning, the organization might be divided in a fierce competition for resources. By Monday afternoon, the VPs might walk out of their quarterly meeting after arriving at a compromise, and the organization might miraculously now be collaborative. This back-and-forth cycle can go on indefinitely as power vacuums are filled with competition.

This multifaceted dynamic of competition is challenging to model because it's constantly changing, unpredictable, and chaotic.

> In my experience competitive chaos leads to organizational chaos.

There are substantial consequences that spring from the chaos. Some consequences can be used positively, and some will need to be combated.

Competitive chaos can be extremely grueling, especially for newer technologists or anyone without intrinsic power or control.

Toxicity

There may be moments when competition becomes so harmful that it's no longer in someone's best interest to persevere through the hardship.

The tech industry has a fascinating way of hurting itself. The ruthlessly competitive nature of the industry inevitably means that there will be intelligent people who end up very hurt. Where there are smart, competitive, and hurt people, there will be toxic behavior.

Toxicity is the degree at which behavior can harm an organization or effort; specifically when the behavior is so harmful action or evacuation is required

Toxic behavior can stem from disappointment, distrust, or—in most cases—organizational dysfunction itself.

A common trait of toxic behavior is its ability to spread to or infect others in an organization. Often a highly intelligent, hyperproductive, competitive, and traumatized person may find comfort in validating their competitive traumas by spreading their obsession with ruthless competition to others.

The consequences of this infectious behavior compound themselves. As people grow and mature in their careers, they begin to predict the toxic behavior and learn from it. In an effort to protect themselves from experiencing another trauma, they might preemptively sabotage other efforts that they see as a threat.

Toxicity is a very real and very harmful consequence of competition. Its effects can be observed directly and indirectly within an organization. And toxicity is, in a way, the antisystem to productivity. The more productive that a person aims to be, when faced with competitive obstruction, the greater the chances that their productivity may turn to toxicity.

Anyone can become toxic.

The more motivated and productive someone is, the more likely they are to become toxic.

Communication (low-context)

Interestingly enough, communication styles can also be linked to competition.

The amount of context given and the number of assumptions made in a conversation can be correlated to competitive thinking.

Low-context communication is communication built on unspoken assumptions and implicit references; allusion

Competitive people often communicate with little or no context offered to the discussion. There's no incentive to offer context within a competitive environment.

Competitive thoughts can be linked to self-centered thinking because self-interest is the primary motivator behind competitive systems. Without incentives to collaborate with others, there's little reason to focus on effective contextual communication.

This type of language can be exceedingly difficult to manage because this language can be almost impossible to understand.

Where there's competition, there will be low-context and unintelligible communication.

Example of Low Context Language

Imagine receiving feedback about her failed idea at the office.

> Your centralized infrastructure idea didn't seem to pan out. Earning your stripes is a big part of the culture here. You spent too much time star gazing and not enough time heads down.

This language is vague, and is relatively unintelligible. There isn't necessarily anything concrete or actionable in this language. The language is based on missing context, and cemented in figures of speech that are liable to be misunderstood or misinterpreted.

This low context language is, unfortunately, normal in competitive environments where the experience of others is de-prioritized.

Applied Hacking

Understanding how competition is relevant to business will help you apply the concepts of competition to tricky problems.

> This is the first time that I'll be applying concepts in the book back to reality and realistic situations. There may be concepts that can be uncomfortable to broach. And there may be concepts that seem unimportant or irrelevant. Pay attention to the examples that seem insignificant or trivial because those may be areas where a privilege can be identified.

Manager Buy-in (Self-interest)

This example illustrates how self-interest can be applied. With the knowledge that those closer to capital are more likely to prioritize their self-interest, we can look at a common problem in tech.

> Imagine that you're an entry-level engineer with very little influence. You're struggling to gain critical buy-in for a technical decision about the product.

The stakeholders believe that it will be better to rush the product to market. The technologists believe that prematurely rushing the product out will create problems for those who work on the product. A decision needs to be made about whether the product should be rushed to market or whether the technologists should be given the time and resources to create an environment to maintain the product.

This is a common predicament for technologists. From the product owner's perspective, the delivery of the technology is clearly the priority. From an engineering perspective, the health of the systems that deliver the technology is clearly the priority.

You know that preposterous product requirements with

undersupported engineering efforts has been a problem. You worry that another hasty product could lead to catastrophic consequences for your team.

You identify that there are two options, and you elegantly lay the options out for everyone to discuss.

- Prioritize the product's deadlines over the system's health.
- Prioritize the system's health over the product's deadlines.

The key to managing this situation is in the framing of the options or how you cast the options.

By realizing that product managers, people managers, directors, and customer-facing stakeholders are closer to capital, you can frame the discussion on their terms.

> **Option 1.** Frame to Their Self-Interest
>
> Cast the option you prefer, in the light of the decision-makers self-interest.
>
> In other words, focus on making the system's health the clear pathway to the perceived goals of delivering the product.

The ability to frame a position in the eyes of capitalism is important. The system is remarkably effective in ensuring that workers learn the lessons of self-interest the hard way.

In contrast, authentic representation can oftentimes be considered dangerous. For instance, this book tries to authentically portray capitalism. Many might consider this book dangerous.

Option 2. Authentic Representation

Frame the options authentically and transparently.

Advocate that the system's health should be prioritized over the delivery of the product. Clearly articulate the crisis that the team is having. Express concern that another delivery-first effort is liable to cause members of the team to leave the company.

The ability to identify these options is a skill within itself. The ability to frame them in a way that influences the outcome is the hack.

The Recommendation

I recommend **Option 1**.

Frame the system's health in the light of product's delivery prioritization. If the decision-maker's goal is to prioritize product delivery, make the case that the system's health is a requirement to the delivery. Depending on how you perceive the decision-maker's posture, it could be advantageous if you were to remove the fork in the road altogether—namely by just fixing the system and neglecting to say anything about it.

Knowing that the stakeholders are closer to capital lets you know that they're more likely to prioritize their self-interest.

And knowing that they're closer to capital also suggests that they're more aligned to competitive thinking. Putting forward that prioritizing the health of a system would offer a competitive edge over your perceived competition could be extremely effective toward winning an argument, if you even decide to frame the argument in the first place.

Use this knowledge to your advantage! Frame the options based on your knowledge of the system.

The Holidays (Self-care)

This example will illustrate how you can exercise self-care by playing by a predefined set of rules.

Societal norms in the United States are very effective at normalizing unreasonable working conditions. In the US, there's a popular expectation to maintain an artificial presence during the December holidays without actually being productive. This is contrary to other locations such as Europe, where many countries will take off entire months, such as August, without any presence at the office. The expectation of an artificial presence at work can be harmful. Personally, I find it disrespectful as well.

> Imagine that you're approaching the months of November and December at a tech job in the US. You sense that these months will be less productive, but you haven't gotten an official invitation from your manager to take time away from the office. You notice senior colleagues (including your manager) less and less. Meetings are starting to get canceled, and productivity comes to a crawl.

This is a common situation that illustrates the complexities with selfishness, selflessness, self-interest, and competition.

Based on the economics lesson earlier, you can look to the fundamentals of capitalism to infer the rules in this situation.

Capitalism expects us to prioritize our own self-interest. Ideally, one would do so without harming others in the process.

Some questions to consider while you consider how to respond to this:

- What are some ways that you could respond to this situation while preserving your own self-interest?
- What are some things that you could do during this time to advance your broader career goals?

The ability to prioritize your self-interest can often feel cynical. It can also be easy to confuse self-interest for selfishness.

Asking your manager to acknowledge the reality of the working conditions around the holidays may be appropriate. The system would expect you to advocate for yourself and prioritize your own self-interest.

The Recommendation

I recommend practicing self-care by prioritizing your own self-interest. Spend your time at the office understanding your career goals. Begin to form plans for how you can structure your environment toward furthering your goals.

Not everyone will have the privilege to be this casual about their approach, but even a few moments of self-care can help.

If your working conditions are working against your self-interest, the correct thing to do is to attempt to mitigate that.

It's important to cut yourself some slack in this scenario: Adhering to the rules of the system and advocating for your own self-interest in this situation isn't laziness or an indicator of a poor work ethic. Adhering to the rules of the system and advocating for your self-interest is brilliant, and you should celebrate it.

So you should say something to your manager and inspire action. Asking to mirror the experience of your European colleagues isn't unreasonable. It's reasonable to take time off during a lull. It's reasonable to be paid for this time off. It's reasonable to ask for the company to respect your time and for them to either use you to your fullest or give you the gift of an honest break.

Bros (Organizational Dysfunction)

In places where competition is rewarded, there will be those who get carried away with the sentiment that competition brings success. When this competitive sentiment becomes unnecessarily harmful, it's no longer productive.

A **Bro** is a term for an unnecessarily aggressive and competitive individual whose actions are counter-productive.

Typically, bros' outward behavior align closely with society's stereotypes of masculinity. But bros typically aren't tactical or strategic about applying their traits of stoicism and self-sufficiency. Without direction and motivation, a wild bro is liable to turn otherwise productive traits inward and damage colleagues who are working toward similar goals.

Despite the masculine connotation of being a bro, I've found bros in every gender. There can be women bros and gender-nonbinary bros. I myself am a trans woman, and I consider myself a bro on occasion.

Bros typically use condescending language and bullying tactics to gain a competitive edge. Bros often unnecessarily compete where they should collaborate, and this competition can be harmful.

This example will illustrate how bro culture can lead to organizational dysfunction.

Imagine that you're hired to work on a specific piece of technology at a company. Shortly after joining, you discover that another department of the company is using the same technology you were hired to work on. You introduce yourself to the other department, and quickly discover that it's a team of hypercompetitive bros.

Right away it becomes clear that the team views you as competition, and the slander and obvious sabotage begins. Before you even have an opportunity to start a healthy working relationship, the problems begin.

Knowing that the bros obviously aren't going away, how do you manage this relationship and hack the system for your own personal gain?

The Recommendation

Remain calm, collect information, and encourage competition under a pretense that serves your self-interest. Take the opportunity to revisit your goals with your position. Consider your overall strategy of what you'd like to accomplish.

- What are your goals at work?
- Do you have technical goals?
- Do you have financial goals?
- What are your goals with the technology?

Bro culture will remain unnecessarily competitive, but you can use this to your advantage by creating a false contest. In other words, bros want to feel like they're winning. Give them a contest to win, and frame the contest to serve your needs. Create an environment so that their victory opens the doors to a greater victory for yourself.

If part of your strategy with the technology involves as much operational work as it does development, create the sensation of a contest for one of the pillars of your strategy. Try to influence the bros to do the operational work by creating a false competition. Structure your work to leverage their work. Have your holistic system bring more value than the operational component that was created by the bros.

In short, try to engage the bros competitively, and use the bro's work collaboratively.

Organizational dysfunction can exist because of competition. But organizational dysfunction is only sustained if the dysfunction benefits another entity. If the cost of the organizational dysfunction is lower than the profit that the dysfunction brings in, then I don't really mind that sort of dysfunction.

By finding the true representation of the organizational subsystem, you can identify how it's relevant to the global motive for profit.

Challenging the organization's ability to remain profitable is an almost guaranteed way to disrupt the organization. And if you feel as I do that organizational dysfunction is sometimes a necessary evil, I think that can offer meaningful insights into how the bros might be affecting the broader machine.

Finally, be wary of toxicity. At some point, the bros might become toxic and infectious. If the bros have crossed the line into toxicity and their actions are no longer worth salvaging despite their harmful consequences, it's time to focus on self-care. Consider your needs. Consider how you can leverage the situation for your own self-interest.

- What part of the situation can you apply to your longer-term goals?
- If it's time to evacuate, is there anything worth doing first?
- Once you make the decision leave the situation, what are your first steps?

If you decide to evacuate, I suggest adhering strongly to the decision. A feeling of certainty in these types of scenarios is often worth the risk of overanalyzing a decision. The longer the decision remains unknown, the longer the situation is liable to inflict damage. Sometimes a quick and possibly less perfect decision is better for triage than a drawn-out and thoughtful decision. Regardless, once you make the decision, free yourself from second-guessing.

Remember, the system assumes that you'll always advocate for your self-interest regardless of your nature or comfort levels.

Conclusion

Competition dominates the tech industry, and it explains the behavior of the industry and those who occupy it.

The tech industry was founded under capitalism, which means that the same techniques that are effective in capitalism are effective in tech.

In other words, you need to embrace competition while also satisfying your own self-interest if you plan to survive. You need to understand that competition and profit are conceptually linked. Where there's a need for profit, there will be competition. Where there's a need for profit, there will be successful competitive personalities, including hypercompetitive personalities.

Be prepared for chaotic competitive culture with extremely low contextual communication styles. Competitive behaviors lead to higher profits. Corporations see this and leverage this. This is why the elite are competitive, self-reliant, and aggressive. Corporations reward competitive behavior, and in many situations they create comfortable landing pads for their highest performing competitors.

In my opinion companies rarely set out to hire only masculine workers. However, many will prioritize profit motivated characteristics in their leadership.

Masculine occupants in the tech industry also seem to have greater faith in competition. This faith can often lead to favorable results in the quest for profit. And while competition may often lead to profit, that doesn't imply alternative avenues such as collaboration can't be as effective.

The industry carves out a comfortable position of influence for these competitive personalities. Focusing on self-interest reinforces this position of comfort.

Not all is lost to competitive bros and superficial self-interest.

Strangely enough, there's a methodology that competes with competition itself.

The methodology of collaboration.

[4] https://en.wikipedia.org/wiki/Worker_cooperative

[5] Harmful masculinity and violence,https://www.apa.org/pi/about/newsletter/2018/09/harmful-masculinity

[6] Nickerson, Raymond S. (1998), "Confirmation bias: A ubiquitous phenomenon in many guises", Review of General Psychology, 2 (2): 175-220, doi:10.1037/1089-2680.2.2.175, S2CID 8508954

[7] https://www.pnas.org/doi/pdf/10.1073/pnas.2111943118

[8] Gender and Competition. Department of Economics, Stanford University, Stanford, 2011

Chapter 3. Collaboration

The antisystem of competition is collaboration. These two components can be thought of as opposite and conflicting paradigms. Because of this opposition, you might be surprised to hear that one of the most effective ways to compete in capitalism is to collaborate.

> **Collaboration** is the process of working together to achieve a common goal.

If a goal is common to one group, there will be opportunity to collaborate toward the shared goal. It may be possible to also achieve a personal goal while collaborating toward a shared goal.

> **Cooperation** is the process of working to achieving one's own goals as a part of a common goal.

There is subtle nuance in the separation of these definitions. Collaboration represents an environment where working together is intended to achieve a common goal. Cooperation however, represents an environment where working together is intended to achieve independent goals.

By drawing attention to the intended goals, it becomes apparent that collaboration and cooperation are similar yet unique primitives.

A collaborative group can often outperform an existing competitor. Where there's competition, there's opportunity to outperform the competition by collaborating. So the abundance of competition in the capitalist tech industry means that there's also an abundance of potential collaboration opportunity.

For every ruthless competitor, there is an equal opportunity to combat that competition with teamwork.

The competitive and collaborative cycles in tech are seemingly never ending. Small instances of competition form inside collaborative structures. Small instances of collaboration compete with less effective competitive forces. The cycle is ongoing.

Similarly to the law of conservation of energy which states that energy can neither be created nor destroyed: only converted. [9] The trend in tech is to exchange competition for collaboration indefinitely. The energy of competition and collaboration is never created nor destroyed, it is merely converted between the two systems. In my opinion the state of the fluctuation of the market is indicative of this conservation of energy.

The contrast of competition and collaboration creates a natural balance between the two opposing approaches. So you can say that the subsystems of collaboration and competition are antisystems of each other. In other words, you can expect to find opposite attributes of one system in the other.

> Competition can be harmful and exhausting. We turn to collaboration to find the opposite conditions.

In other words, all is not lost to the ruthless machine of competition. Collaboration and the components that power collaborative systems are wildly effective at overthrowing the machine of competition. Collaboration can offer refreshment amid the turmoil of a cutthroat capitalist machine. Collaboration can offer kindness where competition can be cruel. Collaboration offers respect where competition offers disrespect. In addition to a refreshing take on the industry, collaboration can flat-out compete with competition. Finally, collaboration isn't possible without the unique people who bring the system to life.

If this book is to equip you to hack capitalism, you'll need to find yourself a reliable group of fellow hackers sooner than later.

Hackers

If one hacker is frightening, just wait till you have a group of them working together. There are tremendous advantages to surrounding yourself with a group of people who you can collaborate with.

> The advantages of a reliable and trustworthy group of peers are far more threatening to an ecosystem than any amount of competitive aggression or ambition.

In competitive environments, the skill of collaborating is often overlooked. Many people within the tech industry grew into their careers with only the skills of competing at their disposal. These types of people effectively overlook collaboration, and they also tend to downplay the advantages of collaborating with others.

This is particularly true with technologists from the United States. In short, the United States does a great job of neglecting to teach the importance of collaboration.

Your average capitalist might ask themselves, "Why would an economy that's built primarily on competitive reasoning and profit-seeking find any intrinsic value in collaboration?"

But because collaboration is often forgotten about, overlooked, bypassed, neglected, or framed as a sign of weakness, you can in many cases use that to your advantage to outperform a competitor. If your goal is to outperform the elite, an extremely effective tactic is to find a group of like-minded people that you can hack the system with.

Concrete examples of these groups include those that support marginalized people!

These groups use tactics such as knowledge sharing to lift up and raise others in the space. These groups work collaboratively, and they offer a respectable adversary to the machine of competition.

> Find a crew.

If no crew exists, create one.

Even if it starts small, its worthwhile to pursue as quickly as possible.

As these groups mature, they form a community. Communities exist everywhere in tech. These groups often surround specific job roles, programming languages, religions, sexual orientations, special interests, specific technologies, and so on.

Community is a group of people existing in the same place while having a particular characteristic in common.

There's a dedicated community of hackers that's free for anyone to join that's centered on the content of this book. We hang out on our Discord server and share our knowledge directly.

hackingcapitalism.io

Make the most of this resource and spend time identifying other resources. Use these resources to meet others to work with. Additionally, consider starting your own and building your own community from scratch.

Trust

For collaboration to work effectively, there must be a common understanding of trust. Trust is the fabric that collaboration is built on.

Trust is the faith in reliability for something or someone

Trust is inherently risky, especially within the confines of competitive capitalism. Trust can bring groups together—or it can be violated and in turn rip the group into smaller divisions.

When a bond of trust is broken within a collaborative system, a form of psychological subdivision occurs and the system divides into smaller competitive systems.

Because of this bond, trust can be used to measure or vet the effectiveness of collaboration. Where there's mutual trust, there's healthy collaboration. Where there's healthy collaboration, there's mutual trust.

Mutual trust lets members of a collaborative community participate without the risk of extortion or danger. Ideas can be shared, and resources can be pooled together.

An absence of trust explains why organizational dysfunction is so abundant in environments where competition is shifting in and out of existence. Competition increases the chances that others will violate your trust to stay competitive. So competition is often built on environments of zero trust.

> **Zero-Trust** is the act of removing all faith from a belief; acting purely on validation and proof.

Collaboration is effectively impossible in zero-trust environments. Collaboration is also an effective way to compete with zero-trust environments.

So some amount of trust within a community must exist for collaboration to work.

This explains why a group of hackers is so dangerous. The hackers have a bond of trust that holds the group together. This trust is the defining factor that separates them from their adversaries.

Knowledge Sharing

As trust is gained within a group, knowledge can be exchanged with little concern of risk. Without trust, there's no knowledge sharing.

> **Knowledge** is information, skills, and methodology acquired through experience.

The ability to share knowledge can amplify the impact a single individual has on their goals. This book is indicative of my decision to take a risk, in the hopes of offering valuable knowledge share.

The most valuable and prized knowledge within the tech industry is much more than the ability to code or craft technology. The ability to apply technology to business is the knowledge that's most often withheld.

Giving away the knowledge of how to apply technology to business is a liability because it can level the playing field within competition. The elite will protect their knowledge, including the fact that it even exists in the first place. This may lead to negative effects such as gatekeeping within the elite.

Collaboration encourages sharing of this valuable knowledge, which can give outsiders an opportunity to outperform the elite. Identifying people to share knowledge with can be alarmingly effective toward outperforming the elite.

> Find hackers who you can trust, and tell one another everything you know.

The more experience that you can combine, the stronger your community becomes. The stronger your community, the higher the likelihood that your community will equip its members to outperform the elite.

Feminine Socialization

In the same way a link can be found between masculine stereotypes and competition, a similar link can be observed with collaboration and feminine stereotypes.

> **Feminine socialization** is a set of ideals that start a young age and defines ideal (or perfect) femininity as related to helpfulness, empathy, humility, and grace. [10]

In the same way language is gendered, I also view behavior as gendered. There are masculine and feminine types, without either one necessarily implying sex, chromosomes, genetics, or identity.

For example a bisexual man may choose to indoctrinate himself into a feminine social framework. The socialization gender has no correlation to the subject's gender.

I believe that feminine socialization directly contributes toward creating collaborative personality types within tech. Where there's a need for collaboration, collaborative people tend to be better equipped for the job, and I've found that more often that not, women are more open to collaboration than men.

But unlike their masculine counterparts, collaborative personality types aren't rewarded or incentivized in the same ways.

Because this subsystem exists within a competition-dominated economy, the luxurious landing pad that you often see for fiercely competitive personalities isn't as common for collaborative personalities. In other words, people with stereotypically feminine traits aren't rewarded with compensation or power nearly as often as people with stereotypically masculine traits.

Thus, we find that women disproportionally carry the burden of collaboration in competitive (capitalist) work cultures. [11]

But collaboration must exist for the system to function. Without collaboration, there'd be no antisystem to offset competition.

The tech industry needs feminine personality types in order to sustain itself, yet refuses to reward them.

There are many factors that contribute to a wage-gap in tech. I am not attempting to offer a thesis that any specific factor is independently responsible for the measurable wage-gap. I am, however, suggesting that my experience has led me to conclude that strongly collaborative and feminine social constructs typically tend to be compensated less.

There is notable research that also concludes that skin color, and sexual orientation also have a measurable impact on pay differentials. [12]\

My observation has been that the underpaid groups in the study have tended towards collaborative or feminine social constructs.

Decision-Making

A decision is only as valid as those that respect the decision, which includes the decision-maker themselves.

The inability to make decisions can create tremendous overhead and turnover within a system.

Decisions are only effective if those decisions are respected and executed. In other words, making a decision isn't the same as influencing people to respect a decision. The two tasks are similar yet very different skills, which is why high-ranking decision makers often aren't the ones who execute their decisions.

Empty decisions are decisions that are made that do not materialize into reality; empty promises; vaporware.

Empty decisions are a sign of competition within an environment. In tech it can be common for stakeholders to challenge one another. This mentality is reinforced with the competitive thinking that a reward will only go to a single winner.

Empty decisions can be easy to detect, and they can have severe consequences.

If decisions aren't respected, they can be challenged. If a decision is challenged, that can lead to organizational dysfunction. Efforts can begin to work against one another, and a company's healthy set of moving parts can come to a screeching halt.

This dysfunction within broader systems can lead to employee burnout, and it can burn valuable resources on necessary work and rework.

Egalitarian decisions are decisions made by a group with the understanding that all involved have equal influence on the decision.

Egalitarian decision-making is an effective tactic for making decisions that are almost guaranteed to be respected.

Letting those who will be affected by the decision have an opportunity to influence the decision creates a higher likelihood that they'll respect the decision.

So egalitarian decision-making can be a way of preventing organizational dysfunction.

Scale

The cumulative effect of collaboration can be astronomical. Even a simple task–if executed in collaborative harmony and at scale–can be overwhelmingly powerful.

Within the tech industry, there can be microeconomies of competition that emerge within broader organizational structures. With every microeconomic bubble of competition comes a new smaller economy. The decreased surface area of these small competitive entities can also be a glaring weakness in competitive culture.

With decreased volume comes decreased resources. With decreased resources comes limitations on an entity's ability to operate quickly and efficiently.

This inability to operate at scale is a weakness with competitive culture. The more competitive an environment, the more fragmented its components and resources become.

Scale is term that describes the volume or rate at which a task is performed

Operating collaboratively at scale lets you exchange resources for a competitive advantage. The more resources that are available, the faster a task can be accomplished.

Even the fiercest and most ruthless of competitors are no match for the speed and power of collaborative scale. Scale lets collaborative forces simply outpace and outperform competitive adversaries.

Authority

With scale comes the need for authority. Authority is the antisystem to influence, which is discussed later in the book.

> **Authority** is the ability to make and enforce decisions or policy

Collaboration **increases the ability to scale**. Collaboration leads to unity and clustering. Groups will join together and form larger groups.

Competition **decreases the ability to scale**. Competition leads to rivalry and division. Groups will break into smaller groups and compete. Authority comes with scale. So collaboration is the fastest tactic to gaining high authority.

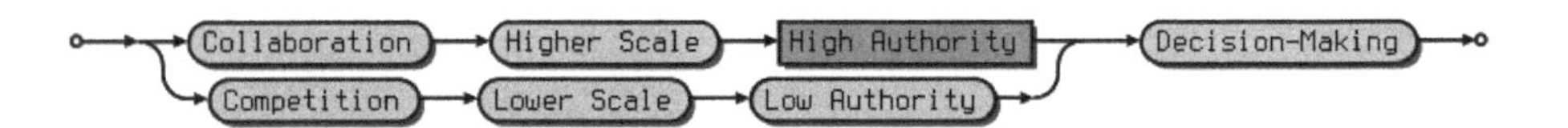

As the number of people who trust the decisions of a system increases, so does the authority of that system. This is a fascinating pattern that's relevant to both humans and computer science.

The Bitcoin technical paper references the concept of a majority proof-of-work in order to validate financial transactions. In other words as long as 51% or more of the computers connected to the bitcoin network agree that a given transaction is authentic: it is. [13]

> In later sections on ethics we discuss the environmental impacts of cryptocurrency in depth. Such as Bitcoin producing 36.95 megatons of carbon dioxide annually. [14]

Search engines have a similar concept known as **domain authority** that describes a website's relevance to a specific subject area based on its scale and use.

Generally speaking, authority can be inferred from trust and scale. The only difference between dreams and reality is how many people trust and believe in it. The ability to drive collaboration and trust will yield a greater authority over decisions.

This is as true for psychology as it is with computer science.

And while gaining authority will help you satisfy your goals, building trust and scale can lend authority to your cause.

Like most lessons in this book, the lesson on authority is equally relevant to distributed computer systems because it applies to people within an organization.

In other words, you can challenge or bypass authority by creating competitive authority.

Brandished Collaboration

The tech industry is built on competition and exploitation. With this ruthlessness comes risk of weaponized collaboration. There can be pressure to collaborate or offer empathy and kindness toward the industry. In my experience this tendency for collaboration can often be criticized or attacked as a sign of vulnerability or weakness.

I refer to this as brandishing collaboration, or weaponizing the technique to discredit the individual pushing for collaboration.

Brandished collaboration is weaponizing collaboration in order to exploit an individual.

In situations where kindness, empathy, patience, and support can be weaponized I often remind people that the tech industry is not their family. Having a reasonable boundary, and a sense of self-respect can be important in preventing weaponized collaboration from damaging your morale.

In systems built on a zero-trust policy, there's inherently a zero-collaboration policy. Without trust, there's no collaboration. If you don't trust a system, you don't owe the system any collaboration in return. Use your ability to assess trust in an environment to draw the line between authentic collaboration and brandished collaboration.

Be wary of any collaboration that isn't built on trust because it's liable to exploit you.

Criticism

Collaboration is the first step towards teamwork. Teams build fantastic things, and create wonderful experiences that can last a lifetime. Intrinsic, teamwork can be a viable tactic to accomplishing goals. Criticism of collaboration can be interpreted as criticism of teamwork, which can be a dangerous position to hold.

There is nothing wrong with teamwork. There is nothing wrong with collaboration.

Both can be effective, if applied appropriately.

However, in an attempt to diminish the value of collaboration the methodologies of collaboration can often be criticised. Hyper-competitive personalities often associate collaboration with weakness. This critical response to collaboration is an indicator of anxiety.

Accept criticism as a compliment.

If you discover that your work is being highly criticized by competitive personalities, that's a strong indicator that your work is effective. Search for criticism of collaboration as a way of validating that collaboration is working as intended.

Nothing is quite as confirming to collaborative hacking as the sensation of competitive people going out of their way to negatively criticize your work.

Communication (high-context)

In the same way that competition inspires low-context language, collaboration inspires high-context language.

> **High-context communication** is communication built on over communicating context in an attempt to transfer as much value and knowledge as possible.

To effectively collaborate, you need to be able to communicate and empathize. High-context communication aims to offer the most insight into a situation so that that knowledge can be shared by the greater collaborative effort.

> Where there's collaboration, there will be effective high-context and digestible communication.

Examples of High Context Language

Imagine that someone received this feedback about her failed idea at the office.

> Your idea to tackle our technical problem with a centralized system to manage our applications was a viable means of addressing the problem. But there were organizational challenges at the centralization approach that were blocked by funding. If your centralization idea could have addressed the problem without the cost overhead it would have been successful.
>
> In the future, there will need to be as much effort put into the cost-risk analysis of driving a solution that goes into the technical aspects. I and other leaders at the company can help with this. Learning to leverage leaders at the company is a good skill to learn to move you closer to a promotion.

Note: This language is collaborative. The language offers plenty of context, and even without developing a setting the situation is clear.

Applied Hacking

Understanding collaboration, as well as its relationship to competition can enable individuals to prepare themselves for difficult situations.

Accessing to this knowledge has been very limited in my experience. This knowledge should be a commodity so that any engineer will be capable of combating the turmoil of competition with collaboration.

Cloud Provider Fragmentation (Trust)

This example illustrates how trust affects the behavior of a collaborative structure in tech.

Imagine that you're working on a project at a tech company that's in the process of moving an application's resources to a cloud provider. The manager of the project is adamant about migrating the entire stack to the cloud, and the team is excited about the opportunity to revisit some of their technical debt.

The members of the team trusts one another, and they collaborate well together as they get into the migration process. Then, in the middle of the migration, the manager announces that they're very unexpectedly leaving the company.

The team is alarmed by the announcement and quickly learns that a member of the team will need to be promoted to take over the project. In the wake of this disruption comes a broken bond of trust.

The collaborative nature of the team begins to fragment, and the members of the team no longer trust one another. The cloud migration remains incomplete while members of the team begin competing with one another for the promotion.

The application remains split between the legacy stack and the new cloud provider, which causes substantial technical problems.

Trust is broken, competitive structures have formed within a previously collaborative system, and the technology takes a dramatic turn for the worse.

This example shows how quickly a single disruption can lead to smaller competitive structures. The team could naturally fragment between the part of the application that had been migrated and the part that hadn't been migrated. The technology took the blow of this psychological system.

These competitive structures are less likely to collaborate without trust. The technology is less effective without the collaboration. The broader system suffered the loss, and the humans found themselves frustrated and burnt out.

- How could someone navigate this situation?
- How could a marginalized person navigate this situation?
- What would be realistic for marginalized people to expect?

The Recommendation

I recommend considering collaborative resources and bracing for the consequences of competition.

While there's no way to predict a disruption such as a manager leaving a company in the middle of a cloud migration, you can look out for the signs and position yourself advantageously in the process.

With the knowledge that trust and scale can influence authority, there's some calculus that can inform you of the best posture to take.

Try to identify two measurements.

- Gauge how much authority you have in the situation.
- Gauge how likely it is for that amount of authority to lead to getting the promotion.

If everyone on the team trusts you, then you likely have high authority in the situation. If the decision to promote someone is based on authority and influence, and the rewards of the promotion are compelling to you, it might be wise to pursue the position. But if your relationships on the team are brittle, then there's very low collaborative authority. This might not be the best time to be ambitious about a promotion.

As a marginalized person, you'll have other considerations as well. Despite your authority and your ability to gain collaborative trust, there still might be problems that will prevent you from seeing an opportunity to be promoted. If the decision makers are biased toward you, they're likely to view your presence as competitive.

In this situation, you can draw on competitive tactics and

resources because their behavior will be predictable. Remember that competition stems from self-interest. Prioritize your own best outcomes.

Collaboration, scale, and authority are your allies in this situation. If the entire team is adamant about your being promoted to finish the migration, it will be more difficult to challenge that authority. Assess the likelihood of your ability to use the competitive difference for your own self-interest.

Unintentional Collaboration with Log4Shell (Authority)

This example illustrates how collaborative techniques created an unintentionally collaborative environment among some of the most competitive corporations.

On November 24, 2021 the Log4Shell vulnerability CVE-2021-44228 was reported by Alibaba Cloud to the Apache Foundation. [15]

The vulnerability allowed for easy remote exploitation on an extremely large number of systems simply by adding a malicious string to various fields that were likely to be logged. If that field happened to be logged, an attacker could initialize a shell and gain unauthorized remote access to a system.

The vulnerability was described as "the most severe vulnerability ever". [16]

As I mentioned earlier in the chapter: With trust at scale comes authority.

Research concluded that 93% of the cloud enterprise environment was vulnerable to CVE-2021-44228. [17]

With this enormous adoption at scale comes an enormous amount of authority. The library affected virtually every publicly traded tech company in the United States because of the amount of trust that they put in the library. This level of trust and authority ultimately led to an unintentionally collaborative system. The entire industry needed to collaborate to survive.

Their trust in the Java library and the resulting authority that the library had on the industry wasn't by design. But the rules of collaboration still applied to this situation. When the various systems of technology that depended on the library were exposed, the cycle of competition and collaboration was disrupted with technology.

Almost every publicly traded tech company was vulnerable to the exploit. A collaborative system had unexpectedly emerged without any culture or prior art. The system was massive and short-lived because there was no incentive to maintain the collaborative system.

Conclusion

Collaboration as a system has delightful results. Collaboration as a tactic can be an extremely effective tool in gaining a competitive edge.

Collaboration is built on trust, and trust is what makes collaboration possible. The refreshing experience of working with peers toward a common goal is only possible with mutual trust. Violating trust will result in smaller competitive systems emerging from the fabric that was once a collaborative system.

With trust comes an ability to share knowledge in the hopes of equipping your fellow collaborators with tools to outperform the competition. Sharing knowledge is only possible with trust, which means that the results of knowledge sharing are only possible by first surrounding yourself with a trustworthy community.

The ability for a collaborative structure to make decisions that are respected and executed is a sign of accomplishment and success. Without a reliable decision-making process, dysfunction and turmoil can occur.

As collaborative structures grow, so does their authority. Collaborative structures accelerate as they grow or diminish in size. They can grow quickly, remain stable, grow slowly, or shrink. As the number of collaborative subsystems that trust and respect the broader system grows, so does their influence. This authority can be a deliberate tactic brought on by clever design. Or in the case of the Log4Shell CVE, that can be the result of an oversight.

Collaboration combats the many points of contention that people have with competition. Because collaboration can challenge competition, it's often neglected or diminished by [NOUN HERE]. Collaboration can offer many positive experiences within the otherwise distastefully competitive realm of technology.

But collaboration isn't necessarily the answer to every problem. Competition also can be valuable as it drives innovation.

Historically speaking, there has been a conflict between altruism and self-interest. Fictional utopian economies that feature communism and capitalism oppose each other philosophically and fundamentally. Novels such as The Grapes of Wrath and Atlas Shrugged have taken grandiose approaches at alluding to one philosophy over another. This contrast has reinforced the thinking that competition and collaboration are antisystems.

When it comes to altruism and self-interest, one isn't necessarily superior to the other.

For every altruistic collaborative ideology there exists a more self-focused capitalist ideology. For every empathetic collaborative ideology there exists a ruthless and harmful capitalist ideology.

But there's a new way of recognizing the speed that these two antisystems work in cycles. There's a grander pattern at play.

Competition can bring about technical innovation. Collaboration can reinforce this innovation as greater scale as resources are applied to the original innovation. This innovation accelerates the rate that humans develop. Ultimately, technology will reset the system, and the cycle will begin again.

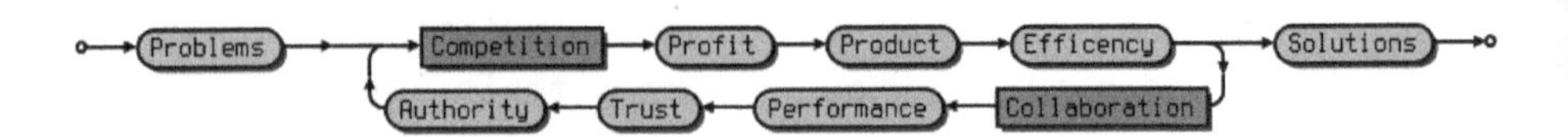

Neither system is right or wrong. There's no binary system because these concepts are two perspectives of a broader system.

They're merely systems of resources. These resources can be understood and consumed.

[9] https://www.feynmanlectures.caltech.edu/I_04.html

[10] Femininity, https://en.wikipedia.org/wiki/Femininity

[11] Gender | In Collaborative Work Cultures, Women Carry More of the Weight,https://hbr.org/2018/07/in-collaborative-work-cultures-women-carry-more-of-the-weight

[12] https://www.americanprogress.org/article/women-of-color-and-the-wage-gap/

[13] Bitcoin: A peer-to-peer electronic cash system, https://bitcoin.org/bitcoin.pdf

[14] https://www.sierraclub.org/pennsylvania/blog/2021/03/environmental-impacts-cryptocurrency

[15] Log4Shell Vulnerability is the Coal in our Stocking for 2021, https://www.mcafee.com/blogs/enterprise/mcafee-enterprise-atr/log4shell-vulnerability-is-the-coal-in-our-stocking-for-2021/

[16] Ars Technica, As Log4Shell wreaks havoc, 2021, https://arstechnica.com/information-technology/2021/12/as-log4shell-wreaks-havoc-payroll-service-reports-ransomware-attack/

[17] Wiz and EY (Ernest and Young), Log4Shell 10 days later, 2021, https://blog.wiz.io/10-days-later-enterprises-halfway-through-patching-log4shell/

Chapter 4. Ethics

The primary goal of most entities that exist under capitalism is to make a profit.

Since capitalism has no concept of moral and behavioral constraints, it is enamored with profits at the cost of human experience.

> A **Code of Ethics** is a guiding set of principles intended to influence behavior and decisions.

Other than profit, governmental bodies and ethics seem to be the only other systems that can have direct impacts on humans that occupy capitalism. The tendency of the system is to veer toward total efficiency by exchanging human resources and technology for profit. Ethics prevent perfect profit-making efficiency in the eye of capitalism.

Ethics is the primary combative force to total profit-motivated extortion.

Ethics is friction in the gears of capitalism. At best, it can slow and deteriorate the machine.

My experience as a transgender woman in tech confirms friction. The machine of the tech industry has confirmed that my search for ethical constructs to protect my civil rights is a point of contention. This is a disappointing truth that often times has been difficult to reconcile.

Learning to identify ethical subsystems can help to protect you while occupying the tech industry. There's no guarantee that ethical subsystems will be present to protect you under capitalism. Trusting that these subsystems will be there is risky.

> Don't trust the system to protect you. You must try to create your own protection.

Because ethics is the primary combative force to total profit-motivated extortion, having ethics in your favor is going to be critical to move you closer to capital.

You need to take ethics seriously.

Corporations need humans to feed the machine. Humans need ethics to thrive. Corporations build rapport by advertising ethics. When there's a conflict, profit will always win over ethics.

This contrast creates a phantom set of ethics—at least on paper. It can be common for corporations to claim that they prioritize a given belief, but in practice, those beliefs are often neglected.

This phantom set of ethics is, unfortunately, is the nature of the system. But you can predict this phantom.

There's first the perceived or overt code that I'll refer to as **The Idealistic Code of Ethics**. Idealism.

This code of ethics is somewhat fictitious. This code exists primarily for official record-keeping purposes. This first code is what the tech industry will try to convince you exists.

The second is the observed or inferred code, which I'll refer to as **The Realistic Code of Ethics**. Realism.

This code of ethics is much harsher, with less consideration to the human experience. But this is much closer to the reality of the tech industry.

The idealistic code of ethics is what you will be able to easily **discover**.

The realistic code of ethics is what you will be able to easily **observe**.

Much like a reconciliation pattern in robotics theory, kernel design, or Kubernetes, you'll often need to reconcile these codes because they often conflict. And you'll likely need to understand both to leverage the system in your favor.

Find the ethical delta.

There will be a resulting gap between the two codes of ethics. The sooner you can identify this gap, the sooner you can leverage the gap in your decision-making process.

The Idealistic Code of Ethics

The idealistic code of ethics is what you can easily discover.

Idealism is projecting a belief onto a situation; unrealistically

Ethics tend to fall secondary to profits. Because of this, they often exist in an unrealistic ideal state. There can be benefits to finding an organization's idealistic set of ethics.

These idealistic ethics will often be posted in various places, written in manuals, or spoken about. Here are some keywords that you might look out for:

- code of conduct
- company values
- guiding principles
- moral values
- organizational standards

Whether the organization is a company, a community, an open-source project, a traditional project, or a function, somewhere at some point—often forgotten about and often overlooked—will be a code of ethics.

Not all these easy-to-find codes of ethics are inherently untrustworthy. Many of them will be taken extremely seriously in the unlikely event an ethical concern were to be raised. And there's a high likelihood that these idealistic ethics will be enforced after the fact. There's a low likelihood that they'll reliably prevent unethical behavior.

You need to be prepared for unethical behavior because capitalism's tendency is to conflict with ethics.

These idealistic ethics will often be easy to find yet difficult to observe.

A famous example of this is Google's "Don't be evil" policy [18] which was reportedly removed in 2018 and is now showing again in 2021.

The policy provides immediate comfort, yet it's almost impossible to reconcile upon closer evaluation. Also known as a "feel good" policy, that has almost no concrete ethical guidance or protection behind it. There are many open questions left open for interpretation:

- What exactly denotes an activity as evil?
- What if one person's definition of evil isn't another person's?
- What if evil is profitable?
- Where does evil stop and profit start?
- Who exactly determines whether something is evil?
- What happens if there's unintentional evil?
- What if evil is a result of their well-intended action?

Typically, these idealistic ethics come in the form of comforting statements that hold little concrete meaning. These statements are designed to make people feel good while simultaneously not actually protecting any specific groups or preventing any unwanted actions.

Idealistic codes of ethics are often rich in language about kindness, compassion, morality, and altruism. Idealistic codes of ethics are also often extremely subjective and subject to interpretation.

Some codes of ethics, however, are more trustworthy while substantially less passionate.

Amazon offers notoriously terse documentation on their ethics. [19]. Their language doesn't inspire feelings of warmth and compassion. But it's relatively trustworthy.

In my experience compassion is rarely trustworthy.

Compassion exists as a necessary evil in the eyes of capitalism. Compassion is a necessary friction.

Codes of ethics can either be honest about this—or not.

Compassion doesn't necessarily generate revenue, after all.

The Realistic Code of Ethics

A realistic code of ethics is easily observed and is rooted in the observation of reality.

> **Realism** is accepting the situation as it is, regardless of how the situation is otherwise portrayed.

Unlike an idealistic code of ethics, the realistic code of ethics won't be written down or posted anywhere. So you must model it independently based on your observations.

Unfortunately for newcomers to the tech industry, you'll usually discover the realistic code begrudgingly after it's too late to recover from the harmful effects of trusting the idealistic code of ethics.

So the only code of ethics worth trusting is the realistic code of ethics that you discover on your own based on observation.

> Model reality before trusting ideology.

The tactic that I use to identify the realistic code of ethics is to research and observe conflict within an organization. The goal is to become well versed in observing ethics. Be diligent. Take excellent notes. Learn as much as possible.

There's no shortage of conflict in the tech industry. This means there's no shortage of data that you can draw from to hone your perception of the organization's realistic ethics.

One tactic to take away from this section is that you should write things down. Diligently noting observations is the first part of effective scientific research. If your goal is to prepare a working ethical model based on reality, that begins with collecting data.

> Start collecting data immediately.

History to Find Deltas

The technique that I use to reconcile a company's realistic versus idealistic ethics is to research and analyze conflicts in the organization. You can research almost any situation, and you can arrive at an ethical delta.

- Find a conflict.
- Research it.
- Understand the dilemma.
- Model the intent, and impact.
- Understand the real nature of the system.
- Understand the ideal nature of the system.
- Determine the delta, if it exists at all.

By drawing on these situations of conflict, you can quickly find a more realistic and trustworthy code of ethics. By uncovering realistic and undocumented ethics, you can navigate situations substantially more effectively.

Comparing the ideal ethics against the realistic ethics will help you understand which ethical principles can be trusted and which can't. Looking at the two codes side by side gives you a one-to-one comparison of each principle. I've even gone as far to create two documents with the same formatting for each code. One based on reality and the other on what I could find.

By finding the delta between implicit ethics and explicit ethics, you can see how off base the company's working culture is from reality. Once you have a more realistic view of the situation, you can more easily understand how to respond to difficult situations.

Emotional Labor

As you uncover the void between an organization's idealistic code of ethics and its realistic code of ethics, you might be concerned about what you should do about it.

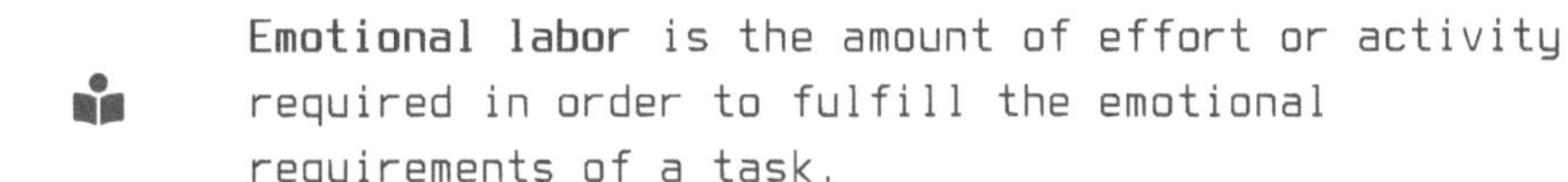

> **Emotional labor** is the amount of effort or activity required in order to fulfill the emotional requirements of a task.

The emotional labor required to address the void can be monumental. Because of capitalism's heavy tendency toward profit and self-interest, there's almost no incentive to dedicate resources to offset the emotional labor of this void.

So the void persists.

In many cases, the void becomes so disruptive that someone will be forced to decide between accepting the impact that the void has on them or taking on the labor to address the void single-handed.

While noble, putting in emotional labor to address the void is almost never aligned with fiscal self-interest. Most of the return on investment for the emotional labor comes in the form of human experience. From a profit perspective, this human experience is necessary operational cost.

> There's no incentive under capitalism for corporations to work ethically, other than the constraints of law, one's own moral code, and the consequences of one's actions. Offering the emotional labor and fighting for the ideal code ethics to match the real code of ethics can be emotionally rewarding, but I think you're better off prioritizing your self-interest.
>
> Emotional labor of this sort pays no dividends in cash.

Ethically speaking, this situation is catastrophic.

The only times when companies prioritize the human experience over profit under capitalism is when they're uncharacteristically generous (such as by putting together a summer picnic for employees) or when someone is pushed past their ethical breaking point. Or-of course-when something happens that disrupts public perception.

The organization maintains their false set of idealistic ethics to keep people under a false sense of comfort. In situations when the disparity becomes too obvious, the organization might shift its realistic ethics to more closely align with its idealistic ethics - or at least temporarily.

Responsibility

Despite being lucrative-or perhaps because of it-the tech industry can be harmful.

The tech industry's dangers can be found in many directions. Whether the industry has an impact on you, on a corporation, on a group of people, on other industries, on the environment, or any other setting, there will be a question of responsibility.

Is the tech industry or its occupants and leaders responsible in any way for the resulting damage?

Responsibility is the obligation or duty to take ownership of a matter.

I think that the primary ethical concern in tech is deciding whether the industry is ethically responsible for its actions.

The United States, for example, is well known for taking minimal action to hold profit-driven corporations responsible for any of their damaging operations. This absence of action is a highly criticized aspect of free markets and free enterprise

In 1970 Milton Friedman published an essay in the *New York Times* titled "A Friedman Doctrine: The Social Responsibility of Business is to Increase Its Profits" where he essentially argued that a corporation has no obligations to society. He also wrote a book titled *Capitalism and Freedom* that includes this perspective:

> there is one and only one social responsibility of business-to use its resources and engage in activities designed to increase its profits so long as it stays within the rules of the game, which is to say, engages in open and free competition without deception fraud. [20]
>
> – **Capitalism and Freedom, Milton Friedman**

Friedman's work obviously favors profit-motivated capitalism. According to Friedman's philosophy, corporations have no responsibility for any harmful consequences of their actions. Friedman is also credited for his work on shareholder theory or stock theory-also known as the Friedman Doctrine.

The shareholder theory has had significant impact on the world according to a 2017 article in *Harvard Business Review* by Sarah Cliffe. [21] Friedman's work is highly criticized for being morally wrong despite its impact on corporate profits today.

The argument, while alarming, does unfortunately exist in today's society, and I personally feel that it's valid. And because many companies follow Friedman's reasoning, the tech industry has embraced a murky ethical sense of responsibility.

> It is often unclear if tech corporations assume societal responsibility. My experience has taught me to assume they do not, even if they claim they do.

Company Loyalty

There's a popular sentiment that employees should remain working for corporations for extended periods of time despite their experience or market trends, even if their loyalty doesn't directly benefit them.

> **Company Loyalty** is the sentiment that an employee has a moral obligation to remain loyal, or stick with a company over time.

The concept of company loyalty is morally absurd within the confines of capitalism.

In many cases, company loyalty is a blatant scam, and it can be in workers' best interests to change jobs whenever they're looking for a promotion to stimulate and compensate for their careers!

> From what I can see, getting promoted at a big tech company is roughly four times harder than getting that job at another company. [22]
>
> – **Corey Quinn, Chief Cloud Economist at The Duckbill Group**

If there's any takeaway from the earlier chapters of this book, it's that capitalism will prioritize self-interest over ethics. The sentiment that employees hold any ethical responsibility to companies is deceptive and hypocritical. I feel that this is particularly true because I don't think that corporations hold any responsibility to act ethically.

Company loyalty exists to motivate innocent workers into positions of exploitation.

Job Hopping refers to the often negatively perceived behavior of changing jobs frequently

Companies might portray job-hopping as a toxic or worrisome trait for employees. Because if employees seem unstable or volatile, they're less valuable to the company.

But in my experience, job-hopping is an extremely strong indicator of future successes.

At-will employment is a well-known United States labor law that states an employer is able to dismiss an employee at any time for any reason without warning.

[23]

In other words, companies can legally fire you at any moment without cause.

In the United States, the implications of losing your job are catastrophic and include becoming unhoused and losing access to healthcare.

The concept of company loyalty is manipulative and deceptive in a capitalist economy. I'm of the mind that employers have no ethical responsibility to society, so I also think that it's unreasonable to expect employees to act ethically toward employers. This is particularly true for societal concerns. If corporations have no responsibility to uphold a quality of life for society, then society also wouldn't have a responsibility toward the quality of life of corporations.

So if you're working in tech, I think you make self-interest your top priority.

Making wise career choices in tech in the 2020s is dramatically different from making career choices in the 1960s or 1970s.

> In my opinion there are situations that call for job hopping. Prioritize your own self-interest.

Remember, the system will seek profit at all cost and annihilate anything that obstructs its quest for profit. If you don't advocate for yourself, the system will exploit you. There's nothing wrong with leaning into the tech industry's competition. If another company is willing to pay you more, treat you better, or offer a better or more comfortable working experience, then it's in your best interest to take advantage of that.

Remember: The tech industry expects competition because the tech industry is built on capitalism.

There's legally nothing wrong with playing the same game that the corporations are playing.

Consequences

At a high level, the ability for a corporation to operate without accepting responsibility for the consequences of its actions is, to put it lightly, alarming. And although it's alarming, this behavior is legal and often encouraged.

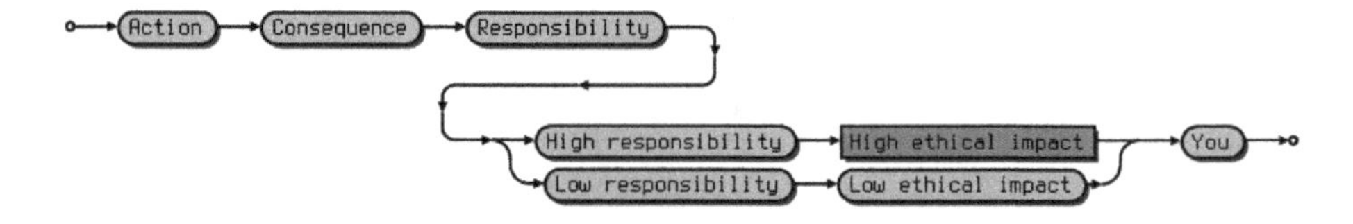

No matter which superficial and intellectual wrappers the economic system uses to justify this behavior, it still remains adolescent at best. Our economic system deliberately lets corporations operate freely without intervention, despite the harms of their actions.

For instance, social-media services offer at best an idealistic set of mission statements, corporate values, codes of conducts, and rules of engagement to offset their harm to society. These superfluous write-ups are the only artifact standing between complete profit-driven extortion and even a small amount of respect and dignity for their users.

For example, in October 2021, Frances Haugen a former Facebook insider, first agreed to a *60 minutes* interview, and later testified before the United States Senate.

> The result has been more division, more harm, more lies, more threats and more combat. In some cases, this dangerous online talk has led to actual violence that harms and even kills people… [24]

Haugen illustrated through her testimony and interviews that Facebook knowingly favored profit despite Facebook's harm to society.

This is worrisome because as far as the philosophy of Friedman, capitalism, and free enterprise are concerned, Facebook's behavior is permissible. Recall that the Friedman Doctrine, which has a substantial effect on businesses today, puts forward the idea that corporations have no obligations to society.

The University of Cambridge's Centre for Alternative Finance in January 2022 estimated the total annualized electricity consumption of the Bitcoin network at roughly 139 TWh (terra-watt hours). [25]

In 2018, MIT's Center for Energy and Environmental Policy Research performed an independent study using hardware from recent IPO filings.

> We show that, as of November 2018, the annual electricity consumption of Bitcoin ranges between 35.0 TWh and 72.7 TWh, with a realistic magnitude of 48.2 TWh. [26]

The lowest metric for annualized energy consumption of Bitcoin is roughly 35 TWh (35,000,000 MWh)

According to the United States Energy Information Administration in 2020, the average annual electricity consumption for a U.S. residential utility customer was 10,715 kWh (10.715 MWh). [27]

	TWh	MWh	kWh
MIT Total Annualized Bitcoin *2018*	3.5×10^{1}	3.5×10^{7}	3.5×10^{10}
Single U.S. Home *2020*	10.7×10^{-6}	10.7×10^{0}	10.7×10^{3}

In other words, going by the **lowest** estimated measurement, the annualized Bitcoin network in 2018 consumed roughly the same amount of electricity that three million US homes did in 2020. Which means that the **highest** estimated measurement brings the total number of equivalent US homes to well over six million.

> We further calculate that the resulting annual carbon emissions range between 21.5 and 53.6 MtCO2; a ratio which sits between the levels produced by Bolivia and Portugal.

The data illustrates that there's a substantial energy footprint-and carbon-emissions footprint-from the Bitcoin network. [28]

This amount of energy consumption and carbon emissions is nontrivial, and it has obvious implications on the sustainability of the planet.

According to the realistic ethics observed, Bitcoin's carbon emissions and its harm to the planet aren't the responsibility of the corporations or of the people who contribute to it.

Therefore, in my opinion, Bitcoin and the people and corporations who participate in its network have no ethical responsibility to the planet.

This is a stark contrast as obviously I feel that we all as inhabitants of Earth have a moral obligation to the planet. Sustainability is critical to our survival. In my opinion the realistic ethics observed with Bitcoin aren't idealistically ethical. Bitcoin is a danger to the planet, regardless of what profit or the flawed realistic ethical construct has to say about it.

To illustrate this further I compare the word *ethical* to the word *moral*.

> **Morality** is the guiding principles that distinguish between right and wrong; good and evil.

In my opinion the definition of ethics as defined in the U.S. law, the Friedman doctrine, and implicitly the tech industry is fundamentally broken; with Bitcoin being the most glaring example.

Bitcoin may, on paper, be considered "ethical". However, due to its impact on the sustainability of the planet, I find Bitcoin repulsively immoral.

Just because something is profitable, does not make it moral.

Conclusion

The quest for profit inevitably has consequences. In situations like Facebook's and Bitcoin's, these consequences amount to unsustainable climate impact and direct connections with harming and even killing people.

The void of legal constraints in free-market capitalism means that companies will routinely neglect to assume responsibility for the problems that they create. So private owners tend to optimize for profits rather than assuming responsibility for the harmful consequences of their actions.

What this means to you in the tech industry is that in any situation where ethics and profit are in contention, the safe bet is to assume that profit will win. And if acting ethically is important to you, it'll ultimately fall to you to build and maintain your ethical principles.

> Leverage the tactics in this book to build a safety net. Protect yourself from the unethical reality of the industry. Build a support network of companions. The industry will not provide one for you.

This is further compounded because the tech industry will likely neglect to assume ethical responsibility for its actions. Spending time identifying the ethical disparity between a company's idealistic code of ethics and its realistic code of ethics can inform other decisions. This can help you develop strategies to increase your influence within a company.

Emotional labor is a form of labor. Which means that the system will see it as an operational cost. So companies won't care about emotional labor unless it's directly linked to profit. And because the labor isn't a requirement of the job, it won't be paid.

Remember, not only will you be the one performing ethical emotional labor, but you can expect to not be compensated for it.

Within the depths of this ethical machinery there's a grotesque takeaway. Companies don't prioritize kindness, compassion, empathy, or humanitarianism anywhere in their ethical models. Capitalism is purely a profit vehicle.

You have to prioritize what's best for you. The days of company loyalty have come and gone. At this late stage of capitalism, the only exposed machinery that's left is a well-lubricated and well-hardened extortion vehicle.

Protect yourself. Nobody else will do it for you.

[18] Alphabet Investor Relations, Google Code of Conduct, 2021, https://abc.xyz/investor/other/google-code-of-conduct/

[19] Amazon Investor Relations, Code of Business Conduct and Ethics, https://ir.aboutamazon.com/corporate-governance/documents-and-charters/code-of-business-conduct-and-ethics/default.aspx

[20] A Friedman doctrine The Social Responsibility Of Business Is to Increase Its Profits, https://www.nytimes.com/1970/09/13/archives/a-friedman-doctrine-

the-social-responsibility-of-business-is-to.html

[21] The CEO View: Defending a Good Company from Bad Investors, https://hbr.org/2017/05/the-ceo-view-defending-a-good-company-from-bad-investors#the-error-at-the-heart-of-corporate-leadership

[22] https://twitter.com/QuinnyPig/status/1484071572314804224?s=20

[23] At-will employment, https://en.wikipedia.org/wiki/At-will_employment

[24] Here are 4 key points from the Facebook whistleblower's testimony on Capitol Hill, Technology, https://www.npr.org/2021/10/05/1043377310/facebook-whistleblower-frances-haugen-congress

[25] Cambridge Bitcoin Energy Consumption Index, https://ccaf.io/cbeci/index

[26] MIT Center for Energy and Environmental Policy Research, https://ceepr.mit.edu/wp-content/uploads/2021/09/2018-018-Brief.pdf

[27] United States Energy Information Administration, How much electricity does an American home use?, https://www.eia.gov/tools/faqs/faq.php?id=97

[28] MIT Center for Energy and Environmental Policy Research, https://ceepr.mit.edu/wp-content/uploads/2021/09/2018-018-Brief.pdf

Chapter 5. Money

Money is the fabric that binds capitalism together, and so money is the fabric that binds the tech industry together.

> **Money** is a verifiable record that is accepted as payment in exchange for goods or services.

Without money Capitalism would not have a means of measuring profits. Without money the tech industry would have no motivation to innovate.

Profit isn't necessarily the definition of Capitalism. There is nuance in speaking about money. There are some situations, such as growing an organization, where profit might not be the desired outcome as proceeds are reinvested back into the organization as quickly as they are received.

A more nuanced framing is speaking about revenue streams directly. Revenue may or may not have a relationship with a profit.

> **Revenue** is the amount of income generated by an entity, ambivalent to profit.

Like most problems in the tech industry, the concept of money begins relatively simply. But when a seemingly simple construct is applied across a vast and distributed set of humans, problems amplify quickly.

With scale, comes complexity.

You can gain a deeper understanding of money by gaining a deeper understanding of what it's used for. You can also find striking similarities between how money and economies are managed and how the tech industry manages the production process.

To do this, let's explore the subcomponents of capitalism and how they relate to common delineations in a tech company.

By tracing the concept of money through the subsystems, you can see the flow of the machinery of business.

> **The Production Cycle** is the holistic system of business that will exchange a product for money, and invest the money back into improving the product.

The Production Cycle Overview

Money is threaded through the production cycle. Money is exchanged and reinvested back into the cycle. As money flows past various subsystems, you can evaluate them.

The production cycle is a nested cycle in a broader system. In the case of large corporations, each production cycle might be independent of other production cycles.

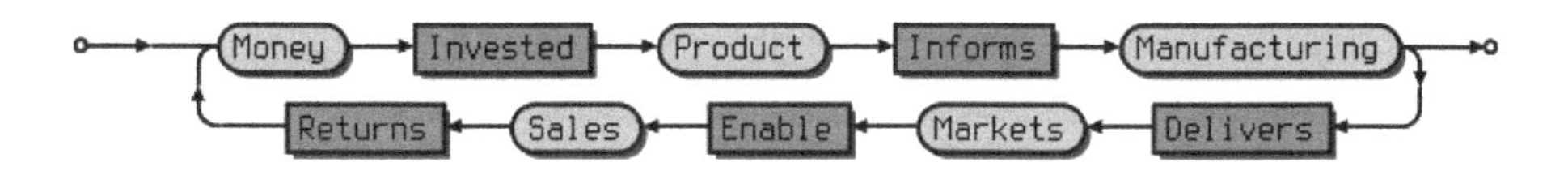

1. Money is invested into product development.
2. Product informs the manufacturing process.
3. Manufacturing delivers a product to be marketed.
4. The markets enable sales.
5. Sales return money (revenue).
6. The cycle begins again.

For example, a product's manufacturing process could far exceed the cost of its marketing. And in that case, it would take the entire system to generate profit. There are trade-offs and consequences to this system. To understand its effects, I'll break down each step in detail.

Production

Creating, maintaining, and manufacturing something of value is ultimately what creates profit.

Production is the process of manufacturing for consumption.

The term *production* is more than just the dedicated cloud account that the operations team has access to. The concept of production is at the foundation of economies under capitalism, including the tech industry.

The means of production, or which entities are responsible for production, define the various economic systems in the world. In Capitalism, the means of production are organized by private owners. In other economic systems they are managed in other ways, such as the government or royalty.

In Capitalism **private owners** control the means of production.

You should understand that production in the tech industry stems from the concept of production in economics, and the elite typically don't give any thought to the humans, computers and software that work to make production happen. They view production as a small economic problem that needs to be managed.

Markets

On the edge of production is a market.

The artifacts of production are only relevant if there's a platform to exchange them for money.

A Market within Capitalism is a system in which consumers and manufacturers exchange goods and services for money.

And like most things in capitalism, the practice of bringing production's artifacts to a venue to sell has been thoroughly thought out and turned into a profession of its own.

Marketing is the process of promoting, advertising, and selling the artifacts of production.

Markets and marketers have a direct relationship with production.

What this means to the tech industry is that if you're working on a production system, your nearest subcomponent in the machine of capitalism will be the marketing department! Or if you're in the marketing department, the gears that turns the marketing department will be the production systems that technologists build and maintain.

For one reason or another, the tech industry does a decent job at obfuscating this relationship. Perhaps technologists perform better when they exist under the delusion that their production systems aren't funneled directly into the hands of marketing just so that everyone can get a paycheck.

Sales

A startup wouldn't be complete without resident salespeople busily watching over and working toward the success of the sales department and incoming revenue.

In order for an entity to turn a profit the amount of revenue must exceed the amount of operational expenses.

This is where the salespeople enter the scene.

Sales is the concrete process of exchanging money for a manufactured product.

Selling a product, can take a tremendous amount of work and requires special attention to detail to be effective at the process.

This is especially true for high-cost products such as business to business products.

A **Salesperson** is an extension of the term salesmen; someone responsible for selling manufactured products.

I often refer to them as *"sales bros"* because of the bro culture that is often successful in these situations.

In the same way that the economy has rewarded competitive personalities in higher level business management, competitive personalities are also rewarded within the discipline of sales. Therefore, there is a higher likelihood of finding those that were masculine socialized within the trade.

In my experience a salesperson does not always have to be masculine or a sales bro. Albeit that certainly has been the trend I have observed. My advice is to be aware of the bro culture with regard to sales.

If you find yourself in a position where you need to maintain a relationship with a sales entity there is a high likelihood you will inadvertently need to maintain a relationship with a group of sales bros. This can be problematic for some marginalized folks who aren't as comfortable existing in the stoicism of bro culture.

Production manufactures products. Marketing brings the products to market. Sales sells products.

By seeing the machinery in this context, you can use this example to correlate more complicated systems. An understanding that the goal of a production system is to help to sell things using marketing can simplify the even the most overwhelming distributed compute layer.

It doesn't matter how badass your production system is—ultimately, production is a vehicle for the sales bros and the marketing department.

At least, under capitalism it is.

Product

Since capitalism's goal is to generate profit, or at least drive revenue, those who run businesses see a clear need to drive up the value of the products. And the more valuable their products, the more money they can sell it for.

In the same way that tech companies employ specialists to bring things to market, tech companies also employee specialists to come up with identify ways to increase the value of their products.

Product refers to the process of designing and developing a system such that it can be sold; the ability to design a manufacturing process and the artifact of the process

The term product also can refer to the deliverable, or artifact.

A single **Product** is the artifact itself; the outcome or deliverable of a production system.

And it's the product team's job to design something of value to sell and to influence the production system that will create it.

What this means is that somewhere in the system someone needs to advocate for what they believe will bring value to the manufacturing process. A healthy production system stems from an understanding of what the manufacturing process should be making.

Product sits at the opposite end of the manufacturing process. If marketing is the step after production, product is the step before production. Marketing and product are adjacent to manufacturing in business.

Understanding this dependency chain can tell you where organizational dysfunction can stem from. Production systems can be damaged if there aren't clear definitions and expectations of which subsystem do what.

Product development influences production, and the cycle begins again.

An unattractive reality for many passionate technologists is that they exist as smaller components in the system of capitalism, which is anything but glamorous.

Despite what any large tech corporation might say, their employees' code probably isn't intended for anything more than generating profit. So as a technologist, your ability to write code and build products that can help generate revenue will affect your compensation.

The Capitalism Paradox

A look at the boundaries of self-interest within business can illustrate a fascinating paradox. Where does the boundary of self-interest lie?

- Independently with each worker?
- At a broader organizational level?

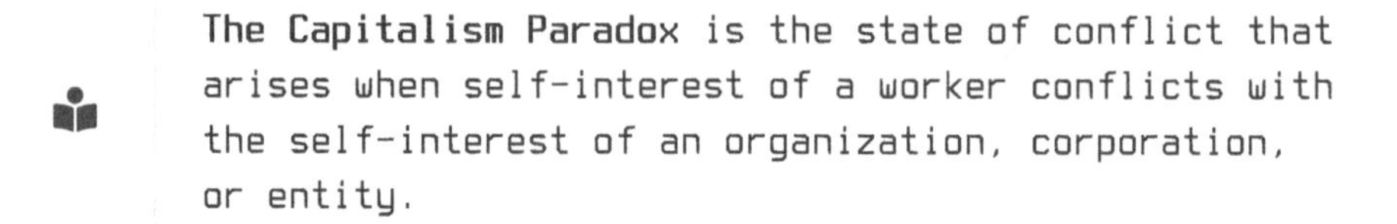

The Capitalism Paradox is the state of conflict that arises when self-interest of a worker conflicts with the self-interest of an organization, corporation, or entity.

So where the boundary of self-interest is drawn or what the definition of self is affects each worker's experience.

On one hand, if the boundary of self-interest is drawn at the organization's level, then the organization's best interest will need to be prioritized over each worker's best interests.

On the other hand, if the boundary of self-interest is drawn at the personal level, then the best interest of every worker will need to be prioritized over the organization's.

Consider perfect systems under each condition:

If the boundary were to be drawn at the organizational level, then workers would merely exist as a means of production in exchange for money. Complete worker extortion would immediately follow.

But if the boundary were to be drawn at the personal level, there'd be little incentive to work for anything less than total share of the outcome. Organizational collapse would immediately follow.

The paradox illustrates that some amount of worker experience and some amount of compensation will need to be exchanged to sustain each entity. The more ruthless that capitalism becomes, the less likely it is that workers will have their experiences or compensation taken into consideration.

What this means to the tech industry is that most tech workers will exist as operational costs in the cycle.

> If you bring your passion to work, then your passion is at risk of becoming a means of production within the machinery of Capitalism. Without access to realistic equity in production cycle, your passion will likely be exploited. Nothing more. Nothing less.

Compensation

I often look at compensation as a goal to get closer to a fair portion of the available funds in the production cycle. That goal, unfortunately, will likely never be reached. But it's possible to try to minimize the difference between a perfect outcome and reality.

Depending on the breakdown in the manufacturing process, compensation can fluctuate substantially. And depending on the complexity and the age of the technology required to manufacture a system, the pool of talent that the company can draw from can become exceedingly small.

A limitation on potential workers and high-value product-manufacturing differentials can yield high compensation. This fact alone is what makes tech such a desirable career path for many technologists.

> **Compensation** is the amount of money exchanged for performing work

In the case of software engineering, compensation is directly tied to the production and manufacturing of products. In the case of marketing, sales, and product, compensation is directly tied to their systems.

In light of the capitalism paradox, neither the organization nor the worker will have perfect compensation from either of their perspectives. The amount of money flowing through production and how much of the production process you'll be responsible for is the most literal way to think about your compensation.

If you can understand where your compensation comes from, you'll understand what your compensation should be.

Unfortunately, the broader ability to understand compensation is often more complicated than just an hourly wage or the amount of salary.

> **Total compensation** is the amount of base pay such as salary in addition of any benefits such as stock, bonuses, commissions, insurance, leave, etc

Understanding that some elements of what many employers and employees consider "part of a package" are created just so they can be potentially withheld or harped on later. For instance, the belief among companies that health coverage or adequate time off are somehow benefits and not requirements is ethically questionable.

But as I concluded previously, capitalism has no obligation to assume responsibility for ethics.

> Healthcare is a problem for the United States because it's structured to confuse, frustrate, traumatize, and–in many cases–bankrupt people. Taking health coverage into consideration for total compensation adds complexity and risk.

Capitalization

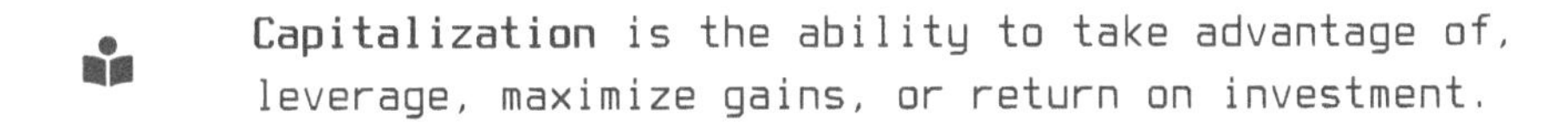

> **Capitalization** is the ability to take advantage of, leverage, maximize gains, or return on investment.

Sprinkling product development and manufacturing on top of an investment to yield higher returns on that investment is the name of the game when it comes to capitalization.

The ability to create value with manufacturing technology is what the tech industry is founded on. Whether the product is a service or a handheld device, the manufacturing cycle is built not only on compensating workers less than the value that they can extract from workers but also on creating value with technology.

> If companies can't capitalize on technical value, then the only way that they can stay in business is to pay workers less than the value that they bring to the company.

Corporations measure their ability to capitalize with money. In the same way that the profit system is a matter of money in and money out, various parts of the production cycle are similar. Companies ask themselves questions like these:

- What is the perceived value of the subsystem?
- What does the subsystem cost to sustain?
- What is the margin between the two? How much do I make on top?

What this means to workers in the tech industry is that if you want your salary to go up, you need to be able to show that your work will generate revenue for the company. So you need to bring more to the table than what you make. The more you can offer, the more you can ask for.

Demonstrate capitalization.

The Consumer Conflict

In the same way that the self-interest boundary presents a paradox for workers in an organization, it can also create a conflict of interest between manufacturers and consumers.

It's in manufacturers' best interests to make products as cheaply as possible. But it's in consumers' best interests to demand products of as high a quality as possible.

The Consumer Conflict is the conflict of interest that arises when a manufacturer and a consumer benefit from opposite product conditions

In November 2006, Microsoft completed the then-new operating system Windows Vista after several years of delays. Vista was released to consumers in January 2007, two months later.

I consider the project one of Microsoft's biggest product failures. The operating system is criticized as consumer hostile and is cited with unreasonable hardware constraints and perceived slowness compared to its predecessor Windows XP. [29]

Windows Vista suffered a protracted development time of between five and six years. And there have been countless technical critiques relating to digital-rights management, performance, pricing, security concerts, and user experience. [30]

Windows Vista illustrates the consumer conflict.

While it was in Microsoft's best interest to produce a feature-incomplete and cost-effective operating system, their neglect for quality and attention to detail came at the expense of very frustrated consumers.

This is a well-known consequence of capitalism. Some organizations will prioritize quality over profits. Some organizations will prioritize profits over quality.

Different types of organizations can yield dramatically different working experiences. If you can gain an understanding of where an organization sits on this spectrum, you can get a feel for the working environment and the organization's culture.

> Product quality offers insights into working environments

In exchange for a higher quality product, you can assume that you'll have to pay more. If your goal as a tech worker is to earn more, working at a company that values quality over cost can often mean that there will be a larger pool for your compensation to draw from.

> More expensive products usually means more compensation for workers.

Worth

In capitalism, there's little opportunity for work to be anything more than extortion. You're worth more than your compensation.

In the same way that there's a disparity between a company's realistic ethics and idealistic ethics, there will also be a disparity between what you make and what you deserve. You can think about your value in the same way that your car's window sticker lists a claimed miles per gallon, which may well be different from your car's actual miles per gallon on the road. So it comes down to measuring the difference between reality and what's on paper. You can do this same exercise with your worth versus your compensation.

> **Worth** is the evaluation of a person's time or an objective value

You should be able to regurgitate your worth at a moment's notice.

You should also understand that it'll be nearly impossible to be paid what you're worth, especially under the ruthlessness of capitalism. So just focus on getting your compensation close to your worth.

There's a formula that you can use to calculate what you're worth per hour.

Your worth (worth) is equal to your total compensation (compensation) over time (time).

For example, suppose that you earned $100,000 a year and that you worked 2,080 hours each year. You can work out that you earn roughly $48 an hour.

```
worth = compensation / time

time = 2080

compensation = $100,000.00

worth = $100,000.00 / 2080

worth = $48.077.00
```

For quick math, you can round the formula to use 2,000 for time. This offers simpler mental arithmetic because you just need to move a decimal around and then divide by two. [31]

So a 100k salary would come out to roughly $50 an hour.

```
worth ≈ (salary / 1000) / 2

worth ≈ ($100,000.00 / 1000) = 100

worth ≈ (100 / 2) = 50

worth ≈ $50.00
```

This is an imperfect model of your worth, and most financial advice would encourage you to never measure your worth or charge based on time. However, having an idea of where you are can help you prioritize your time. I suggest not to charge by your worth, but rather use it as a way of prioritizing your time. Your worth is a signal that can be leveraged in determining if something requires your attention or not. Your worth is not a way of setting how much compensation you should earn.

Time is a finite resource, thus measuring and charging based on time will imply there is a maximum amount you can earn. In other words, don't charge by the hour: charge by the project.

In physics, we often frame formulas as exchanging one value for another. For example a commercial jet can exchange altitude for velocity. As the plane climbs higher, the velocity slows. As the plane dives lower, the velocity increases. This ability to trade altitude for velocity allows pilots to easily calculate their cruising altitude and trade it for speed.

You can also exchange time and money using some quick math.

For example, suppose that you're worth $50 an hour, and it costs $40 dollars to have your laundry done by a service. From a strictly financial perspective, if you were open to and able to find some freelance work that you could do during the time when you'd normally be doing laundry, it wouldn't be worth your time to spend any more than an hour doing your laundry.

There will also be times when this structured model of the world could prevent you from paying for things that you would otherwise. For example, the idea that you should never spend more than you earn within an hour for something that lasts an hour would imply that you should never spend more than $50 on an hour-long meal.

Ultimately, time isn't money—or at least it shouldn't be.

Directly linking time to money is a way to limit your potential earnings. Developing a healthy understanding of your worth, compensation, and time can offer a higher quality of life.

Debt

I think it's obvious that the initial investment into product development has to come from somewhere. If you have no products to sell, where would the investment into the first product development come from?

> **Debt** is money that is owed; the obligation to return the money

Money that's borrowed will typically be paid back with interest.

> **Interest** is additional money paid back at a particular rate for the use of borrowing money.

Interest and debt have devastating consequences, particularly on the working class and those who don't have the education or resources to work out of debt.

The concept of unbalanced debt and economic enslavement is so well understood from a historic perspective it has a specific name.

> **Usury** is making unethical, or immoral loans that knowingly unfairly enrich the lender.

In many historical eras, including in Christian, Jewish, and Islamic societies, usury was illegal. [32]

In my experience today's laws around debt are less humane than in prior eras. I think the usury problem is sufficiently getting worse.

As you recall from my lesson on ethics, you know that you can't trust the system to provide ethical protections.

So it's in your best interest to assume that all debt under capitalism that knowingly enriches its lenders is immoral.

As you may know, technologists also have to struggle with

another type of debt.

> **Technical debt** is the outstanding cost of needing to rework, or reconstruct a system that was put into place by prioritizing cost over quality.

What this describes is the practice sometimes used by technologists of borrowing from the quality in exchange for taking on technical shortcomings. And like monetary debt, technical debt also compounds greater with time. Where there's technical debt, there's also technical interest: technical usury to the systems.

The interest within a technical organization is the pressure to deliver a timely product. With the pressure to deliver a product, comes the need to make sacrifices in the name of time. Often times these sacrifices need to be remitted later, and thus technical debt is occurred. The longer the debt remains unaddressed, the worse it becomes.

But not all debt is intrinsically harmful. Tech is a small industry with a lot of money.

As technologists and entrepreneurs demonstrate an ability to generate revenue with small initial investments, these initial investments can become quite attractive to anyone looking for a high return. These investments are typically very lucrative. Within the context of the global markets, the tech industry is a fast-paced industry with high risk, and high reward.

Venture Capitalism

Like most things in Capitalism, the concept of bootstrapping a corporation will obviously unfairly favor the elite.

Venture Capitalism offers a strong and compelling opportunity to propel an idea to the status of the lite with external funding. Organizations can get more done with a strong team, and some starting funding.

The trade of identifying product and manufacturing ideas to fund the initial production cycle is known as *investing*. Those who invest in companies for a profession or for the venture are known as *venture capitalists* or simply *investors*.

> **Venture Capitalism** is a form of private equity and financing that investors offer startup companies to begin their first production cycle.

Effectively, venture capitalists are investors who invest for trade, profession, or in some cases joy.

A venture capitalist will provide funding to kick off the production cycle for a newly formed corporation or startup. A venture capitalist might also influence product or invest in product areas that they have an interest or experience in.

In exchange for their investment into the production process, a venture capitalist will own a portion of the process. This ownership will be represented with stock.

Stock

I also thank my illustrious friend Milton Friedman-who taught that corporations have no responsibility for their actions-for his influence on modern stockholder theory. [33]

> **Stock** is the shares in which the ownership of a corporation or company is divided; common stock.

Stock is arbitrary: Shares are divided so that they're meaningful to whoever creates the stock. Under capitalism and capitalist societies, most people are legally allowed to form corporations or form their country's equivalent entities. When a company is formed, the person who's forming it selects how many stock shares there will be. The number is in many cases quite literally a fill-in-the-blank-style text field on a form.

- It could be one thousand shares; a million shares.
- It could be one share to every dollar.

- It could cost one share to every cent.

As the company earns more money because of the production cycle, the value of the company is divided by the shares of stock.

In a simplistic model, each share is then worth its proportional value of the corporation.

Like most things in the system, there are exceptions and complexities. There are different kinds of stock, and venture capitalists also have a preferred style of stock that's coincidentally named accordingly.

> **Preferred stock** is a unique class of stock that may have a combinations of features, equity, and liability unique from common stock.

What this means to you in the tech industry is that the investors and founders of the company will typically deal in preferred stock. You'll likely deal in common stock.

Post-Economic

I have decided to include a section that defines the term *post economic* as it illustrates the mindset of many members of the elite in tech. Understanding this framing can be critical, despite it's otherwise ruthless nature.

As a marginalized tech worker, it will be important to understand how those you depend on think, so you can position yourself for success.

> **Post-economic** is a term used to describe a personal financial state where compensation is so high that economic pressures no longer exist.

I first heard this term while working at Microsoft. I also heard colleagues of mine who worked at a nearby Google office use the term.

This concept is extremely controversial. This book in no way is suggesting that anyone needs to achieve that level of wealth to be considered successful.

To be in a position in which the economy no longer has a control or an effect on your life is in many cases a fantasy. The economy will always have some effect on your life, regardless of your wealth. If anything, your relationship with the economy will need to be greater based on the amount of wealth you achieve.

Despite being a fundamentally flawed goal, the term post-economic is indicative of a construct within capitalism that I'd like to draw attention to: The ability to escalate above the lower class of tech workers.

The elite understand these constructs, and they embrace and celebrate them.

I was astonished when I first made the discovery that the elite understood these concepts, understood the consequences, and simply didn't care. In fact, the sentiment that I observed was the opposite of what I would've expected. The elite were proud of their aspirations to post-economic wealth. They were proud of their goals, and they often overlooked their harms in their wake. They seemed to forget about the fact that their wealth came at others' expense.

Applied Hacking

Understanding the production cycle and the intricacies of money, stock, compensation and worth can be complicated.

In this section, I go over some common situations that technologists may find themselves in. Applying these realistic scenarios against the framework of the production cycle, ethics, and capitalism can give some fascinating results.

Understanding an offer

Unfortunately, the ability to understand whether you're getting paid what your worth is quite complicated. Not only are there many factors that go into total compensation, but understanding how that compensation is valued against the production cycle can be challenging, if not impossible. You might be asking yourself questions like these:

- How does somebody make sense of a job offer?
- How exactly does someone understand if a particular job offer is adequate or not?
- How much are your options, healthcare, and total package actually worth?

In this example, I'll ignore paid time off and insurance by design. Imagine that you were to get similar job offers for the same senior-level technical role at publicly traded tech companies.

So let's suppose that the first offer comes in, and you pull these details out of the offer letter.

Offer 1

Salary	Bonus	Stock 4 year cliff
$175,000.00 yearly	$100,000.00 on hire	$200,000.00

Shortly after, you receive a second offer letter designed to be competitive with the first offer. You distill similar (but somewhat different) metrics from the second offer.

Offer 2

Salary	Bonus	Stock 4 year cliff
$155,000.00 yearly	$35,000.00 yearly	400 shares

At a glance, it might appear that the first offer is clearly more exciting. But on closer investigation, you might find more information. To truly compare the two offers, let's represent all values using **the same units**:

	Yearly salary	Yearly bonuses	Yearly total
Offer 1	$175,000.00	$100,000.00*	**$175,000.00***
Offer 2	$155,000.00	$35,000.00	**$190,000.00**

Because the first offer comes with a one-time bonus of $100,000, it may seem like it's obviously a higher offer. But by understanding that that bonus is one time and that the second offer pays four bonuses of $35,000, you can tell that the second offer will actually pay more by the end of the year.

To get a better feel for what the stock may be worth, you could even spend some time researching each company's stock price and its performance over time. Each company will have a four-character ticker symbol, and you can easily research them to find information such as their market cap and stock price.

In this example, let's suppose that your research shows these stock prices, and you broke the packages into yearly installments:

	Stocks granted	Stock price	Yearly total
Offer 1	500 shares	$100.00	**$50,000.00**
Offer 2	100 shares	$1,000.00	**$100,000.00**

By comparing the value of shares against the current stock price and placing the offers in a table, that breaks them down into yearly payments where you can see the packages' finer details:

	Yearly stock	Yearly salary (with bonus)	Yearly total compensation
Offer 1	$50,000.00	$175,000.00*	**$225,000.00***
Offer 2	$100,000.00	$190,000.00	**$290,000.00**

Stock can fluctuate as the production cycle goes up and down, and let's suppose that a quick bit of research on both companies' history shows that their stocks are at all-time lows. Which means that it's likely that they'll either both go up or that they'll both tank.

Laying the offers out with the same units and the same timeframes yielded fascinating results. Despite the first offer having an exciting first-year payout of $325,000, it'll go down to $225,000 a year later. Once you translate from stock price to valuation for both offers, it becomes clear that the second offer–despite being made of all lower numbers–is actually substantially better.

I would choose the second offer.

And despite being a clearly favorable offer, I'd also spend time gauging the total compensation amount against its perceived value in the production phase. Let's say that a conversation with the hiring manager were to allude to several million dollars in available funds for production. If there's only one other person on the production team, where's the rest of the money going? It's probably going to–you guessed it–the higher-ups.

This basic understanding of the production cycle and your position in it can have a monumental effect on your ability to negotiate your salary.

Conclusion

Money is the antisystem of production.

These two paradigms are reflections of each other. They conflict with each other. Production wouldn't exist without money. Money wouldn't exist without production. The ability to turn some amount of money into more of money is where production enters the equation. The better a corporation is at production, the more money the corporation will earn. This is the nature of capitalism.

There are many personas and subsystems that bring a production lifecycle into motion. The role that you'll play in a tech company will affect you where in the production lifecycle you sit. Production is a means to an end in the broader dystopian capitalistic machine.

Your worth is by definition more than your compensation.

In fact, for the production cycle to exist, the capitalism paradox reminds us there must be tension between your compensation and the company's quest for profit.

Production will endlessly cycle through itself time and time again, and new production cycles can be bootstrapped by investment. Venture capitalists will continue to compound their investments, and corporations will continue to pay workers less than they're worth. Debt will continue to financially abuse people, and corporations will unfairly motivate and traumatize workers.

These lessons aren't cynicism. This is just how capitalism works.

Being prepared for and having a realistic understanding of these subsystems can save decades of learning the hard way.

Corporations—by design—won't reward you enough to promote you to the next level in the system.

The reward will need to come in other ways. The reward needed to move closer to the elite has to come through cleverly engineered hacking tactics that are external to your compensation and your traditional work.

So money alone isn't enough to privilege-escalate yourself to the elite.

[29] Windows Vista, https://en.wikipedia.org/wiki/Windows_Vista

[30] Windows Vista, https://en.wikipedia.org/wiki/Windows_Vista

[31] TANIWHA, Taniwha's Applied Napkin Index for Wage by Hour Algorithm, @taniwha

[32] Usury, https://en.wikipedia.org/wiki/Usury#History

[33] The Friedman doctrine, https://en.wikipedia.org/wiki/Friedman_doctrine#Influence

Chapter 6. Building

Whether you're manufacturing technology, breaking into a bank's infrastructure (ha-ha don't actually do that), or positioning yourself for a promotion to vice president, you'll need to be able to turn ideas into reality. You'll be responsible for not only developing and maintaining systems but also designing systems that are so effective that they can combat extortion.

You'll need to be able to build-and you'll need to be able to do it well.

> **Building** is the process of creating, manufacturing, engineering, or otherwise constructing something.

And there will be many beautiful people in the world who enjoy building and creating things.

> A **Builder** is someone who builds.

By trade and by passion, I've always been a builder. I feel lucky that my passion has been able to take my life as far as it has. Building matters because it can be applied to a vast number of concepts. Each of these concepts can be used to help you grow in title, income, influence, and ultimately grow closer to the elite and the capital.

No matter what you're building, your ability to do it well and methodically is a pattern for success in the tech industry. Those who build well have unique opportunities to pursue their dreams.

The anxiety under capitalism is very real.

There seems to be an ever-present longing for more while never being able to satisfy that need in a world structured around money, labor, and work. Building gives builders opportunities to address this anxiety. Building gives builders opportunities to take action and turn ideas into reality.

Building can turn dreams into reality, and it can also be used tactically within capitalism. You can use building to competitively outperform others under capitalism.

The book has already made use of my building ability.

For instance, in the chapter on money, I built a small graph to convey the bottom line during salary negotiations. Likewise, I built an ethical model based on economics to show the differences between ideal states and realistic states. I went over models that compare competition to collaboration, and I discussed the implications of language in each model. The book itself is a reflection of my desire to build a resource that will equip people from marginalized groups with the tools and resources to help them outperform their peers.

An ability to build efficiently can sometimes offset the advantages that non marginalized people have over people from marginalized groups. In other words, there may be peers in the tech industry who have had a head start in their careers, but in some cases, building can help to offset those head starts. These will be people who may be white or male or straight who perhaps were also born into situations with access to higher education, money and other resources. Your ability to build will support quick problem solving and competitive results. You can use these results toward your goals, dreams, and self-interest.

Anecdotally, I've built other systems in my life:

- I've built a system to get dressed in the morning without waking my partner.
- I've built a system to reduce mud in the house when the dog comes inside on a snowy day.
- I've built systems for climbing mountains.
- I've built distributed Linux systems for my career.
- I've built systems to help find high-paying jobs in tech.
- I build systems to build connections with people I love.

Some might even say that I have a building problem. Building has been a way for me to apply economic and technical machinery to my life.

When I discovered my fear of public speaking, I started a Twitch stream. When I discovered my overwhelming amounts of debt, I built a program to help me manage my finances. When I discovered my lack of access to healthcare, I built an HTTP scraper to help me hack the medical industry.

The more I that practice building, the better I get at it. This has taken years. There are several preliminary steps that you need to have the hang of before you can consider yourself comfortable.

If you can build comfortable systems, you're demonstrating an exceedingly competent understanding of the skill of building.

You'll need this competency to hack capitalism.

Obviously, the system is set up to maintain its stronghold over workers like you. So I'll teach you how you can apply the building process toward your goals.

The Building Process

There's an iterative process that I use to build things.

This process typically sits underneath the manufacturing step in the broader production cycle. Replacing manufacturing with the building process can connect the building process to product development, sales, and marketing.

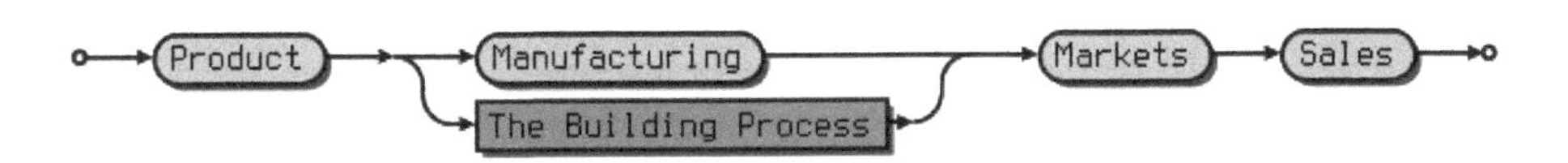

1. Make it
2. Make it work
3. Make it work well
4. Make it work well for you

I think of the first steps of the building process as a way to ease into building for a problem. And I think of the final steps of the building process as a way to ease into applying to a solution. The building process is a bell curve with the peak right at the sweet spot in the center.

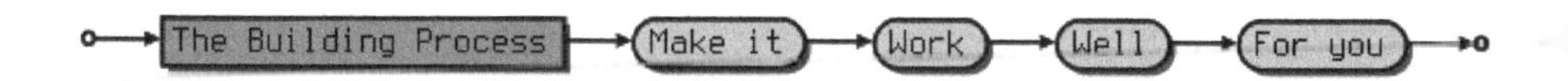

No matter what I'm building, the process remains relatively the same. In some situations, some interior steps might be more or less substantial depending on the situation. But the overall process remains the same. There's an important prerequisite to the building process, which is the design phase. I sometimes think of the design-or architecting-phase as step zero.

If you stick to some rigidity in the process, that allows for some freedoms. And if you understand the goals of each step, you can complete each step without having to worry about the outcomes of other steps. For example, you know that optimizing, or making something work well, is out of scope for steps one and two. So during the first two steps, you can forgo any form of optimization without worrying about effects. Understand the nongoals for each step.

In other words, start simple.

Gall's Law

A complex system that works is invariably found to have evolved from a simple system that worked. A complex system designed from scratch never works and cannot be patched up to make it work. You have to start over with a working simple system. [34]

Make It (Setting)

This step matters because it'll **establish a setting**.

The most important step in building something is getting started.

In many situations, there can be tedious planning and preliminary work that goes into the building process. But building a working model will force you to set up a working environment.

> **A Prototype** is a preliminary model, system, or machine from which production forms are developed, copied, influenced, or replicated.

Building a prototype of something will establish the setting in which more work can be preformed later.

In software engineering, I typically view this phase as creating a new software repository and building out a small "hello world" style program. This critical step will force the hand of small decisions that can not only have an impact on the future design but also speed up the development process.

This step will offer a place. And it creates a space dedicated to the development of your project.

For instance, while building a small software project, there are ancillary considerations that will be resolved right away.

- Where will development take place?
- What license will the software begin with?
- What are the implications of the development environment?
- What name should you give the project?
- Who has access to the project?
- Who will the project's existence interfere with?
- What will be the organizational outcomes of even starting a prototype?

In other situations, this preliminary process can come in the form of just trying something that seems like it might work. I often see technologists refuse to try something out of fear that they'll do something incorrectly. On the other hand, I also see "production" systems built on top of prototypes that never make it past the first stage of the building process.

My suggestion is to lean hard into the *make it* phase.

> Never underestimate the value of making a new directory, creating an empty GitHub repository, starting a new empty Google Docs document, or buying a new domain.

Sometimes the notion of *we are starting* is enough to completely change the paradigm of how a project is considered. This can affect your own mind as well as others. There seems to be a dramatic shift between *we'll start soon* versus *we've started today*.

So my suggestion is to let go of concerns about the other phases of the system and just try to have fun with this phase. This phase should always be somewhat enjoyable.

In addition to offering a safe space for development, you can also use this simple step as a bargaining chip. In difficult engineering conversations, the idea of dramatically changing an existing system can be a difficult conversation to have. Referring to a small prototype that they might consider can remove some intensity as compared with the prospect of a strict replacement. Use prototyping as a way to organizationally tiptoe into a project.

The primary takeaway of this phase of building is to establish a setting.

> **Boilerplate** is necessary utility that needs to be solved before any innovation can begin; the necessary requirements before action and innovation can begin.

Take advantage of prototyping for boilerplate. You can innovate later.

When you're done with the prototype, you should be able to step away from your project. This phase is complete as soon as you establish a setting, and you've successfully created what will soon be your first thing.

At the prototyping phase, the project should *not* work. The project should be relatively wonky, for lack of a better term. It should work enough to show something is possible. It doesn't need to be polished.

I suggest that you start the prototyping phase as soon as you can, especially if the consequences are low. I propose that you start this phase at the same time that you're making decisions, designing, and dreaming.

Make It Work (Proof)

This step matters because it'll **establish proof**.

This is the phase that will take you from a placeholder prototype to the first working contraption.

Offering a preliminary safe step between this phase and the design phase can free you from having to do mindless clerical chores when the moment strikes.

So the timing of being able to get a system working is a rare moment. It often comes without warning, and it can disappear as quickly as it arrives.

There are many reasons to take advantage of the moment. Perhaps a design meeting finally gave enough detail into the project. Perhaps you had an unusually inspiring amount of coffee that morning. Perhaps you had a good night's sleep or perhaps a poor one.

The point is you want to be comfortable when the innovation strikes. There should be little standing in between going from your established setting to established proof other than your own innovation.

In the same way that the first step can free the builder from later considerations, you can also use this step in a simplistic way. Having an extremely fundamental goal gives you an objective to build toward.

> **Definition of Success** is a simple way of determining if a system is working.

I often have very simple definitions of success that guides my building process. Some example definitions of success that allow for reliable building:

- I can run a single command, and a web server will run on my local system.
- I can push a button on my phone, and my car will start.
- I can see how much my stock is worth at a moment's notice.
- I can turn off the espresso machine from an airplane.
- I can run a single command to list all listening TCP ports on a remote system.

The point isn't to get to lost in the details–you can address those later.

The primary takeaway of this step is to achieve the definition of success or prove that the system can do what it's supposed to do. In many cases, identifying the definition of success is worth more than the actual prototype at this point.

At this phase, your project should work. You should be able to prove that the concept is feasible.

I suggest that you take the time to consider this phase delicately. This is the only phase that seems to be difficult to time correctly. When the moment strikes, it's best to be ready for it.

Make It Work Well (Efficiency)

This step is important as it will **establish efficiency**.

Efficiency is how you trade technology for time and something finite such as money. The ability to build *efficient* systems is how you'll trade the limited resources that capitalism provides for systems that can outperform others at your level. So if your peers all have relatively similar paychecks, responsibilities, and free time, your ability to build efficient systems is how you'll outperform them.

Remember that competition is the basis of capitalism.

Trying to make something work efficiently can also prove or disprove your approach. While an initial working prototype might satisfy the definition of success, it'll likely be offensively inefficient.

> Success Endurance is the ability for success to endure small and quick changes in an approach.

Perhaps the most important result of the prototyping step is that you'll have a working system.

You can then introduce small changes to the system. If you built the system well, it should be easy for you to demonstrate success or failure after each small change. Keeping the success cycle small lets you make dramatic changes over time.

Ideally, the prototype at this point can easily show success while it gets more efficient with each change.

At this point, the project should begin to work well. Here's where user experience, resource efficiency, usability, and other systems-design principles can begin to be considered.

In the same way that a definition of success lets you quickly check whether your system is working, a definition of efficiency can let you quickly check whether your system is as efficient as you need it to be.

> **Definition of Efficiency** is a simple way of determining if a system is working as well as it needs to be.

You'll need to understand this step when I apply the building process to capitalism. You will need to be efficient in your career, and with your relationships with people.

Make It Work Well For You (Return)

This step matters because it'll **establish return**.

A good system works.

A great system works well.

A smart system works well, and it addresses a specific need in the process.

In the same way that you can use a definition of success to check whether your system works, and you can use a definition of efficiency to check whether your system works as well as it should, you can also use a definition of advancement to check whether your system is being applied as you had intended.

> **Definition of Advancement** is a simple way of determining if a system is accelerating a cause as was intended.

The truth is that another way that you can think about this step is to look at whether your system can be applied to a problem. For example, an ability to measure how many people travel across the Bay Area bridges each day is a strong indicator of the bridges' abilities to let people traverse the water.

A good builder should be able to advance both their reputation and their system's purpose. But in the case of capitalism, looking out for your self-interest first can be the difference between total and partial extortion.

Some builders will neglect the earlier steps and primarily focus on their systems' abilities to boost their reputations. Tech's builder community has a unique knack for purging those who create deliberately bad systems so that they can't create future systems.

😅 Problems

I absolutely love a good problem, and so should you!

Problems are what power all builders. If it wasn't for a well-defined problem statement, builders would have nothing to build. As an engineer, you should find excitement and joy in collecting an endless list of frustrating problems. There's no need to solve any of these problems immediately–just begin collecting them.

Problems and building are antisystems of each other. Each must exist for the other to function.

Producing technology has a lot of problems. Builders can address problems.

Capitalism has a lot of problems. And builders can address problems.

But having problems is good because they represent building opportunities. Each building opportunity offers the potential for a steady paycheck and an opportunity to advance yourself.

I often say every problem I discover, is the equivalent to finding an unsecured or unpatched server in the wild. Which means finding a computer that can easily be compromised.

Every problem in the tech industry is a vastly underestimated exploitation opportunity with an enormous attack surface!

This is particularly true for highly motivated people, particularly those who've been hurt the most by the system: tech workers from marginalized groups.

Both the tech industry and capitalism have bountiful problems. Which means that builders will have bountiful opportunities to exploit the system.

Architecting

The building process assumes that you've cemented an idea before you've started working on a solution. The process of introducing or designing a system is often an offshoot of architecting.

> **Architecting** is the ability to design a system that can be applied to a specific problem

Architecting comes from a need to solve a problem. In the production cycle, subsidizing a need is up to product design. Another way to represent a need is to frame it as a problem that consumers have.

Where there's a problem, there's a need to address the problem with a system. And where there's a need to solve a problem, there's a need for a design to fuel the building process.

Architecture surrounds the building process! Building comes from problems and designs, and hopefully the thing that you build will be a relevant solution.

A good architect will inspire the building process, and they make sure that the building process leads to a system that addresses the problem.

In the eyes of a tech corporation, architects apply technology to the capital to advance product development.

In the eyes of hacking capitalism, tech workers apply tactics to the tech industry to advance their careers.

Labeling

Labeling is an intellectual skill that you can use to build modular systems because it lets groups easily communicate about and sort components.

> **Labeling** is the process of assigning one or more sets of identifying categories or names to classify something

This book, for example, has heavily used labeling. By adding thoughtful symbols, language, and names to complex ideas, you can use those labels to build and expand on ideas later. For instance, because you have a good understanding of *competition* in the economy, you can easily add new topics, such as aggression, to the competitive model.

Architects and builders can use labeling to think about systems and later components. Once someone creates a label, people can understand what it means. You can focus more time on the labeled components than on defining what a component might do.

Earlier in the chapter, I covered success endurance. The various approaches that led to success can be referred to as *fulfillment options*.

There might be more than one valid fulfillment option in the efficiency process. For a specific problem, you might want to sort the fulfillment options based on speed, cost, or maintainability. By sorting the fulfillment options, you can discuss the trade-offs of speed versus cost.

Labeling makes otherwise complicated discussions much more reasonable.

Observability

In addition to labeling systems for ease of communication, there are times when you'll need to measure parts of a system that would otherwise be difficult or impossible to measure.

> **Observability** is the ability to measure the internal states of a system based on observations of external outputs.

Observability of systems often comes naturally, so it's often overlooked. Many systems don't explicitly include observability features because observability is often a natural outcome of whether the system is working: A broken system is obvious, and a working system is equally obvious. So observability often comes as an afterthought.

For example, imagine a running gas-powered vehicle in a snow-covered parking lot on an early winter's morning. The car will be warm to the touch, and most likely it'll be making the familiar noise of a running engine. The exhaust will be noticeable as it hits the cold air. These "features" of the system tell you about the system's internal state.

But that observability wasn't explicitly designed. That's just how gas engines work. Now imagine an electric vehicle that makes no noise, has no exhaust, and doesn't become warm to the touch. The system's internal state is harder to detect because of its lack of observability.

You don't know the state of the car. It might be running. Or it might not be.

Consider what type of insights would be useful in a system.

Knowing that profit is the primary goal of Capitalism, and that the system expects you to advocate for your self-interest, it can be very advantageous to design systems that are observable. The easier a system to observe, the easier it is to operate. The easier it is to operate, the higher value the system can generate. Thus, higher revenue.

Furthermore, it is useful to offer insights into systems that will enable adoption, usability, and operability with the system.

Operability

As you gain insights into the system's state, you may want to mutate its state. An ability to easily change the internal state of a system is its *operability*. In the same way that you need a steering wheel on a car to affect the drive shaft and the wheels, you also need to make your systems operable.

> **Operability** is the ability to change the internal state of a system based on external peripherals.

An ideal system is one that people can easily understand and easily mutate. Mutations should have an effect, and those effects should be repeatable and demonstrable.

For example, suppose once again that a car is running. This time, there's a button that toggles the engine on and off. You can also easily tell whether the car is running. And you have a button that changes that state.

In computer science, concepts like observability and operability are often overlooked because computer programs aren't as tangible as physical things. In contrast, with bridges or factories or machinery, it's usually easier to understand their states because they have noticeable physical attributes and side effects.

Bridges span water. Factories have lights and sometimes exhaust. Machines usually have moving parts.

I learned these lessons of observability and operability the hard way in computer science. Monolithic programs often came with feature flags that didn't affect the system. Distributed systems would allow for configuration changes, but they didn't require there to be a component to reconcile those changes.

You see observability and operability in software such as Java projects and distributed systems like Kubernetes.

Hostility

Features relating to observability and operability aren't always user friendly.

In many cases, capitalism and profit-oriented programming impede on healthy user experiences.

> **Hostility** is when operability is intentionally taken away in an attempt to maximize profit.

There are countless examples of this in the world and many more in the tech industry. Enumerating these would certainly feel amazing, but that's outside the scope of this book.

- If you can't unsubscribe from a mailing list without first logging in, that's hostile.
- If you can't start a car without having a credit card on file, that's hostile.
- If you can't cancel a subscription without a lengthy phone call, that's hostile.
- If you can't drive across a bridge without first stopping to pay a toll, that's hostile.

As a builder, you'll have a personal moral decision to make.

- Will you allow profit's hostility to get in the way of your system's operability?
- If so, how much hostility will you allow in your system? And where?
- What's your price? How much would it take for you to sacrifice your system's integrity to hostile profit-driven influences?
- What's the trade-off between hostility and sustainability?
- When is it no longer acceptable to risk hostility in exchange for sustainability?

Extensibility

Oftentimes a goal may be clear but the means of achieving it aren't as clear.

While you build systems in tech, there will be many situations like that. An ability to create a clear interface between a broader system and its subcomponent is known as extensibility.

> **Extensibility** is the ability to enable a broader goal of a system by allowing for arbitrary subcomponents to do a portion or all of the work.

Building extensible systems is relatively common in computer science. We've all seen this concept in plugins and add-ons in many of the programs that we use every day. Over time, the markets have shown that having a common interface creates micromarkets that can operate with a product interchangeably. For example, anyone who grew into adulthood into the 2000s is familiar with cell-phone makers shipping proprietary chargers with their phones. The upshot of these proprietary chargers was that it was very inconvenient to charge your phone, and it often required specially ordering an expensive throwaway charger. These cell-phone charging systems were originally very inextensible. But USB–literally the universal serial bus–quickly corrected this inconvenience and brought standardized cell-phone charging ports to the world that we know today.

In the same vein, it can be handy to be able to identify and build extensible systems. An ability to take inextensible systems and make them extensible when growth is a desired outcome is even better.

Many open-source projects heavily lean toward extensibility because that means that different contributors can bring different implementations to the project. A single contributor might bring one implementation, while another contributor might bring another. Because both these contributors use the same interface, their code is easy to swap out when different features or outcomes are desired.

The importance of standards and standardization matters here. Open source and collaborative projects have found value in standardizing the shape and requirements for various extensible subsystems.

In the same way, you can leverage standardization in all that you do.

Bay Area Bridges

While living in Silicon Valley, I became fascinated with the bridges in the Bay Area.

I felt that the bridges were very metaphorical to my work as a software engineer and as an architect.

The three bridges that I spent the most time daydreaming about-from oldest to youngest-are:

- The San Mateo/Hayward Bridge (Opened 1929)
- The Oakland/Bay Bridge (Opened 1936)
- The Golden Gate Bridge (Opened 1937)

Even though the Golden Gate Bridge is the largest, most extravagant, and most famous of these bridges, the San Mateo/Hayward Bridge is my favorite for architectural reasons.

The San Mateo Bridge is the most unsightly and unimpressive of these bridges. The bridge is effectively a thin road spanning a highly unused part of the San Francisco Bay. The road itself sits just above the water. From the air, the bridge appears to be a thin floating road that would snap at even the slightest breeze.

But the San Mateo Bridge was the first of these bridges, which opened in 1929. [35]

> A lightning flash that spanned the nation in the fraction of a second Saturday afternoon opened to the motoring world the longest highway bridge in the world, crossing South San Francisco Bay.
>
> — San Jose News, San Mateo Bridge Opened By Coolidge; Autos Crowd It Full

This was the bridge that dramatically increased the population, money, and economic growth to the downtown area. This growth fueled further projects such as the Golden Gate Bridge.

The San Mateo Bridge was the first bridge in the Bay Area that worked and served as a bridge.

Larger projects like the Golden Gate Bridge wouldn't have been possible if not for the impact of the earlier but less impressive San Mateo Bridge. The San Mateo Bridge was the first viable alternative to taking a ferry.

The takeaway with the Bay Area bridges is that if you want to support elaborate projects such as the beautiful and famous Golden Gate Bridge, you must first start with the simple, economic, and less impressive functional work.

Build the boring bridges first.

Offering a working bridge that did its job of getting people from one side of the land to the other was critical to the success of the other bridges. The City of San Francisco had to manage the funding, the construction, and the maintenance of the first bridge before the other projects were started.

Likewise, your projects should follow the same pattern. Whether you're designing distributed systems, a monolithic software repository, or managing a complex structure of people, you'll need to add support for commerce first. Supporting commerce can be unattractive, but it's necessary.

If you're building a distributed system, start with creating the network and maintaining connectivity of the components. If you're building software, start with plumbing the configuration options and command-line parameters directly through to the libraries.

In the same way that Docker enabled Kubernetes, the San Mateo Bridge enabled the Golden Gate Bridge.

Do the unattractive work first as a gift to your future self and future architects.

Follow suit of the often forgotten about San Mateo/Hayward Bridge.

Remember, successful projects and platforms grow like cities. Organically. Start simple and enable commerce first and foremost.

Infrastructure

There's another interesting paradigm behind the Bay Area bridges related to cost and funding.

Bridge are funded by governments to facilitate commerce. Bridge don't necessarily have a concept of a traditional customer because bridges are built for the common good. The truth is that you can never quantify exactly how much economic growth is directly related to any given bridge. But the evidence of the growth is apparent. The cities of Oakland and San Francisco have been bridged, and so they've forever been influenced by the construction of their bridges.

Infrastructure in tech is similar to bridges because it'll never have a direct customer, and it'll always be relatively hard to connect how much money the infrastructure is responsible for.

To take this analogy further, imagine one of Tesla's modern-day electric cars as a traditional tech product. The bridge lets the car drive from one part of the bay to another. The bridge may be responsible for allowing the transport of some of the raw materials that went into the car. The bridge may even be responsible for helping to transport the engineers who designed components for the car.

The bridge becomes an essential component of commerce. It's hard to map a single product, such as one of Tesla's cars, back to a bridge. This fundamental change in thinking between cost-reducing infrastructure and profit-motivated product is critical to understand while building systems in tech.

Some systems will need to move fast and inspire innovation, such as Tesla. These systems are hungry for profit and their design should reflect this. Other systems will need to move slowly and be as reliable and stable as bridges. These systems are designed to withstand the test of time in a cost-effective way, and they should reflect this.

One high-level goal of a bridge is to minimize cost to the city. The high-level goal of Tesla's car is to generate profit for Tesla.

Because of the change in thinking and the funding differential, the two systems will favor different attributes during their design phases.

Applied Hacking

Wherever capitalism will inevitably try to extort and exploit workers, there will be opportunities to build systems to try to combat that.

Bros (efficiency)

Remember the bros from earlier chapters? These are the competitive masculine personality types who are trying to compete with you.

> Imagine that you're working at a tech corporation and you discover that there's another group who's trying to solve the same problem that you're trying to solve. You're relieved to discover that there's another group who's passionate about the same problem. But after you approach the other group in the spirit of collaboration, you discover that they view you as a threat instead of an ally. They view your presence as hostile, and they start trying to outperform you. The rivalry creates a sense of urgency as they begin to quickly try to rush their solution out the door. Their urgency turns to aggression, and the group starts to harm your position at the company.

It is not impossible to imagine why this type of situation would be common, especially under the extreme working conditions that Capitalism creates.

It's not hard to imagine why this type of situation can be common, especially under the extreme working conditions that capitalism fosters.

The problem is clear: The other group views your presence as a threat, and they're reducing your chances for success. The potential to collaborate with them is lost, and you now face a difficult situation.

- How do you manage the problem of the aggressive bros?
- How do you manage the situation in your favor?

In this situation, you discern that the bros will likely won't have a chance to optimize their systems. They're rushing to get through the second phase of the building process (*make it work*). And you quickly realize they haven't had a chance to focus on the third phase (*make it work well*).

With this knowledge–and a small amount labeling–you can quickly begin to work around the situation in your favor. Knowing that the bros will likely get their system working, you can create a label for this need. Architecting a superset of systems that have a need for the newly created label can open the door for a broader win for your cause.

For example, if the bros were building a deployment system for a specific tool, its label could be the Tool Deployment System. And if you were to design a system that solved a well-known company-product problem while also taking advantage of various Tool Deployment Systems, that would be one way to compound the bros' sense of urgency and redirect their efforts in your favor. While this approach to building might mean that you'd have to sacrifice your original project, it'd certainly exceed at progressing your title and influence.

The Recommendation

Double down on the urgency and harvest the free resources.

You have a problem and you need a *Tool Deployment System* immediately!

Fortunately for you, there's another group at the company–the bros–who are building such a thing. You realize that this represents an enormous opportunity to gain valuable resources at no cost to you. By expanding your plan and making your original design more relevant to the broader production cycle, you can build a bigger, greater, and more applicable utility!

You would do this at the expense of exploiting the bros.

While this approach may seem unethical to some, it can certainly be advantageous to ambitious technologists from marginalized groups.

Not all exploitation needs to be permanently harmful, however. By maintaining a sense of dignity, collaboration, and morals, you can give the bros the opportunity to replace their prematurely released *Tool Deployment System* with a more efficient replacement.

Conclusion

Building lets you replace capitalism's classic lack of resources with technical machinery.

Building and applying systems lets good builders do more effective work with the same or fewer resources. This, unfortunately, is one of the few ways that you can progress toward the elite in capitalism.

The building process supports small iterative changes. With capitalism, your ability to turn limited resources into efficient machinery can be a compelling tactic. This is—interestingly enough—the same tactic that product development will use to advocate for product design.

As an architect gets better at applying systems with elegant designs, a builder can get better at build efficient solutions sooner. Your ability to design more efficient systems will come from your experience with observability, measurability, and operability. And your ability to design more manageable and maintainable systems will also come with experience. I suggest starting to build systems however you can. Whether you're building small hacks around your daily life or among distributed cloud-computing infrastructure, start small and follow the process.

Building lets clever engineers design systems to stretch their resources. But there's also a way that you can create random resources that you can use to exploit capitalism.

Breaking.

[34] How Systems Really Work and How They Fail

[35] San Jose News, March 4, 1929, https://news.google.com/newspapers?id=ADAiAAAAIBAJ&pg=3006%2C6299044

 Chapter 7. Breaking

Capitalism, by design, always limits the resources of those who occupy the system. And when resources are limited, workers are often overburdened. So if you can uncover new resources, that can free up time and energy that you can dedicate to accelerating toward the elite.

Breaking is the act of misusing, stopping, dismantling, wrecking or otherwise rendering a system inoperable.

Breaking lets you introduce resources that wouldn't otherwise exist. I often look at breaking as a way of rolling the dice for resources. There may be more resources. Or there may be no resources. There may be counterproductive consequences.

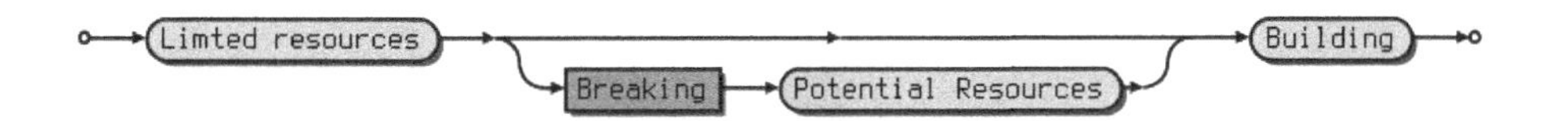

In some situations, having the option to break can be helpful. Particularly if more resources would be helpful and there's little to lose otherwise.

You can also use breaking to validate your building process because it can offer a quick feedback loop.

Every breaking attempt helps you learn something new while making your strategies more resilient and efficient. So the process of systematically dismantling systems is an antisystem to the process of building them.

When systems are built, they need resources. And these resources need to be well funded for companies to make a profit. So where you have systems, you'll have resources. You may be able to harvest these resources in unexpected ways because systems might have unexpected behaviors. And system resources can sometimes also be used for more than one thing.

Any system will exist in many dimensions. Breaking will often expose ways that you can observe the system.

- The system's raw materials
- The system's intended uses
- The system's unintended uses

To break a system, you must first see the system in its many forms.

Breaking can show you where a system will end up. Breaking increases resiliency. The more that you break a system, the more you can repair the system and prevent it from breaking.

Accepting that all systems will eventually break is part of building resilient systems.

Many architects neglect to consider that systems exist in a perpetual state of brokenness.

You can use breaking to manipulate systems in ways that they weren't intended for. In the most literal sense, this book is an example of breaking capitalism and the tech industry. You can use breaking to hack systems or to exploit systems.

You can apply breaking's constructs to the tech industry by observing how the elite respond to breaking. Breaking will expose new resources, new functionality, and new opportunities to you. Where there's carnage, there's opportunity.

Intent and Purpose

Each system has two important elements:

- an intent
- a purpose

You can measure the gap between those concepts not unlike the way that you measure idealistic and realistic systems, compensation, and worth.

 The **purpose** of a system is what it does.

From a builder's perspective, a system's intent and its purpose should coincide. So builders will try to keep the difference between the intent and purpose as small as possible.

An experienced builder will take pride in their ability to design a system that's used as it's intended.

 The **intent** of a system is what it is supposed to do.

From a breaker's perspective, however, the more unintended uses that they can discover with a system, the better.

An experienced breaker will take pride in their ability to uncover unintended uses in systems.

In San Francisco, there are popular windsurfing, kiteboarding, and wind-foiling destinations along the bridges. The bridges provide access to windy parts of the Bay that would've otherwise been inaccessible.

Each bridge's **intent** is to transport people across the Bay.

But to windsurfers, the **purpose** of each bridge may be to provide parking and access to the center of the San Francisco Bay on windy days.

	Goal	Delta
Builder	Intent should match single purpose	Small
Breaker	Intent should not match many purposes	Large

Havoc

Destruction can be extremely opportunistic, and is typically vital to the health of an ecosystem. As resources are consumed, systems break down. As systems break down new opportunities present themselves. Systems can often time be improved, or made more efficient. Often times the broader environment a system exists within has changed with the passing of time. Technology has improved, the constraints of the environment have shifted, and so on. The destruction of old systems can typically make room for new and improved systems in their absence.

Healthy destruction can be observed in nature, business, organizations, and computer science.

Within the observable universe, there's a balance between order and disorder. This balance may span microsized scales to the most astronomical scales.

For example—and perhaps counterintuitively—forests need to periodically burn to achieve sustainability.

> **Havoc** is widespread and overwhelming destruction.

Wreaking havoc is the process of breaking a system as quickly, and destructively as possible.

Destroying an interface is a powerful tactic that you can use to exploit a computer system. These next two concepts are so common and effective that the cybersecurity field has given them convenient names:

> **Fuzzing** is the act of trying to break a system by providing invalid, unexpected, or overwhelming inputs to the system.

Fuzzing is used to demonstrate unexpected functionality that may be used to exploit a system.

> **Destruction of Service** is rendering a system inoperable by causing the maximum amount of long-lasting damage.

You can apply similar tactics to the tech industry, the economy, and your career in tech.

Market disruption is a common goal in business, and when companies can pull it off, it can make for a lucrative investment.

Market Disruption is the process of introducing economic innovation to a market by disrupting the current norms.

An example of market disruption is the ride-hailing industry. Before technologies such as GPS satellites, the cloud, and smartphones, on-demand taxi services existed under a different paradigm. Letting passengers schedule rides based on their locations disrupted the market. Jobs were affected because of the disruption, and new jobs were created. From the havoc of the outdated taxi industry came a new and thriving digital age of ride hailing.

Where there's market disruption, there's room for growth.

Where there's systems destruction, there's opportunity to exploit others.

Where there's chaos in an organization, there's space for influence.

Break shit. See what happens.

The lesson in this section has less to do with the specific techniques of breaking, and more to do with the concept of finding value in breaking in general.

Regardless if you are fuzzing a computer program, or chaotically disrupting a project the tactic remains equally effective.

By identifying weaknesses in a system, you expose opportunity for improvement. With disruption comes innovation.

Breaking is a viable way of instilling innovation in a system.

Debris

From havoc emerges the remnants of a once-operable system. Among these broken remnants are treasures waiting to be discovered.

New and unintentional systems may be created from the shambles of havoc, and those resources might now be available for consumption.

The fallout from widespread destruction is chaotic. But the remains can be useful. Carefully considering the remains of havoc is a skill that's very common in the hacking community.

Learn to look at debris as a resource.

Learn to utilize this resource for your needs.

An astonishing amount of groundbreaking change comes about during emergencies such as natural disasters, pandemics, and war. These disasters break social structures and create opportunities. I think that learning to use these disruptions to your advantage can be extremely dangerous but also extremely effective.

My advice to anyone who reads this is to please use this knowledge responsibly. Using emergencies to achieve your goals can be toxic, harmful, and immoral.

Within the tech industry, there are many situations that can break the current mode of operation. These otherwise frustrating scenarios can often be rich with the debris from chaos and havoc.

For example, it's not uncommon for large tech companies like Google, Microsoft, Apple, and Amazon to rearrange themselves internally.

These unexpected events are known as *reorgs*.

Reorganization or "reorg" is when a large tech company will change some or all of its internal human resource structure.

These reorganizations of human resources can be frustrating to employees because the reorg's debris can cause unexpected changes in employees' working experiences. For example, office initiatives may shift, managers may be changed, and teammates may come or go.

But with debris comes opportunity.

With change may come frustration but also flexibility and loosely defined success criteria for the workers in the *new* organization. The flexibility of this success criteria is important. Depending on your goals at work, there's likely opportunity to advance these goals in the new formless organization. Where there is flexibility, there is opportunity for influence.

A hacker would pay close attention to the debris in these situations.

Take careful and detailed notes of newly forming systems. Observe these systems in their raw forms while they come to life. Exploit any vulnerabilities as soon as you detect them.

> Imagine that there's a dramatic and unexpected reorganization at your company. With this alarming shift, you realize there are many senior-level and management positions available as new positions are opened up to manage the new structure.
>
> You have a realistic expectation that you probably won't be promoted into these newly available positions. And you understand that there'll be tremendous chaos while new management joins the organization.

The situation's debris can feel hopeless, but a hacker can find opportunity among this debris.

If you know that the organization will have technical concerns because of the reorganization, that can be useful to you. The lack of a solid management structure can cause frustration and a low-quality working environment. But a lack of management structure can also offer you technical freedom.

You can influence technical decision-making while there are limited decision makers involved. Structuring these easy-to-make decisions can help you influence the system:

- If your goal is to earn more money, you might structure the chaos toward your expertise.
- If your goal is to earn a higher title, you might structure the chaos toward your ability to delegate and influence others.
- If your goals are to do as little labor as possible and to preserve your mental health, you may want to take the chance to offload some of your chores to a service.

You need to carry a concept of ethics with you as you exploit these situations. It's common for others to view these scenarios as opportunities. But each person's character is defined by their ability to expose these opportunities while also considering the impact to others.

It's easy to exploit a system at the expense of others. It's tolerable to exploit a system with no impact to others. It's skillful to exploit a system and elevate others in the process.

Where there's debris, there are resources.

Where there are resources, there's opportunity to collaborate or compete.

Where there are broken windows, there's opportunity for better windows and in some cases an entirely new structure.

Madness

You should keep in mind the concept of madness as it relates to debris. Or more specifically how madness refers to generating debris.

As someone who struggles with mental health and neurodivergency, this term means a lot to me.

Madness is attempting to mitigate debris with the same actions that caused the debris in the first place

Madness is widespread in the tech industry.

Startups repeat the same product ideas, business models, and market strategies over and over while continuing to fail. But from one effort's debris can come another effort's foundation.

Downtown San Francisco's landscape reinforces this metaphor perhaps too genuinely. There are multimillion-dollar companies forming within the walls of broken buildings. There's poverty, homelessness, addiction, and human waste on the same streets that business executives walk between meetings.

Organizations will find themselves buried in unmanageable technical debt only to apply the same working habits to their reluctant bailout. The madness cycle begins again.

The product team will deprioritize the security team's concerns in the name of turning a profit. Their negligence will cause expensive security breaches in the future. These breaches are fostered by rushing new products to market, and the madness cycle begins again.

Product will de-prioritize security concerns in the name of turning a profit. The negligence will cause expensive security breaches in the future. These breaches are funded by rushing new products to market, and the madness cycle begins again.

Operations teams will be rewarded for responding to engineers' needs. The reactive culture will produce reactive systems. These reactive systems will often be undocumented and poorly designed. Engineers will find problems with bespoke ill-defined systems, and they'll pivot to other systems. Operations teams will react to this shift, and the madness cycle begins again.

Simply pivoting to a new system does not necessarily address the fundamental behavioral problems that contributed to the destruction cycle in the first place.

Remove yourself from the path of destruction in a madness cycle. Position yourself near the path of productivity in a madness cycle. This can be done by influencing the reorganization in your favor. It is possible to identify voids in the organizational structure and adopt a posture of "gap filling" temporarily.

This can be done much more effectively during the chaos of a breaking cycle, than during the stability of a building cycle. Learn to understand the ebb and flow of building and breaking, so that you can take advantage of opportunities as they arise.

Where there is madness, there is predictability. Where there is predictability, there is opportunity to align your involvement with the cycle accordingly.

Deviation

Systems are prone to deviating during a crisis.

When there's havoc or widespread destruction, there's often crisis. Organizations, companies, and even teams are subject to panicking when things suddenly break. During this panic, rules, behaviors, constraints, and system boundaries are often overlooked.

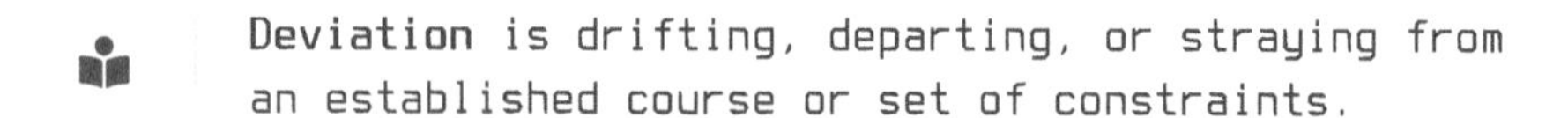

Deviation is drifting, departing, or straying from an established course or set of constraints.

Deviation matters because it can be weaponized. Many will view crisis as opportunity to justify their behaviors that wouldn't otherwise be condoned.

Regardless if deviation is a tactic that is used by you, observed by you, or used against you, it should be well understood.

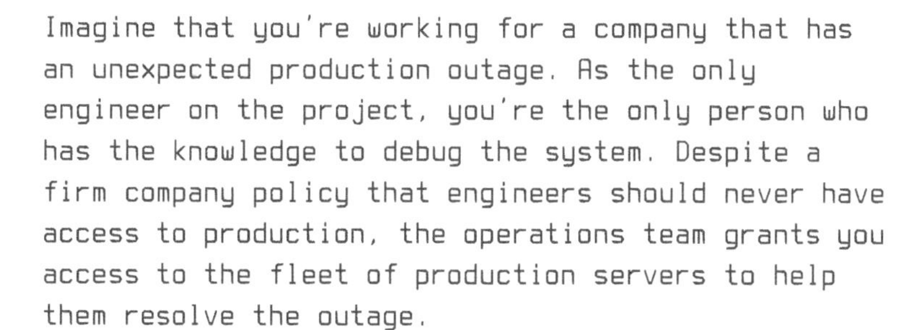

Imagine that you're working for a company that has an unexpected production outage. As the only engineer on the project, you're the only person who has the knowledge to debug the system. Despite a firm company policy that engineers should never have access to production, the operations team grants you access to the fleet of production servers to help them resolve the outage.

In this example, the normal security constraints have deviated. There are many technical concerns with this deviation.

- What if the engineer leaves a backdoor?
- What if the access remains granted after the incident?
- What if there are downstream consequences of this outage fix?
- Will all production be contaminated and need to be rebuilt?

There are also many social concerns with this deviation.

- What happens if there are further unexpected side effects from the methods used to try to resolve the outage?
- Who's responsible for any further damages?
- Does the engineer feel comfortable with their getting access to production?
- Does the engineer even understand the side effects of their having access to production?

Regardless of the consequences, there's something obvious.

- The engineer now has access to production

If that engineer were to be malicious, or they were to have previously tried to gain unauthorized access to production, that would support the notion that crisis and deviation may be a repeatable attack vector.

Where there's crisis, there's deviation. Where there's

deviation, there's opportunity.

The engineer has now discovered a repeatable way to gain access to production.

You can also apply this lesson to how you navigate organizations and the tech industry. Depending on your goals, there may be opportunities for crises to work well for you. For example, the 2020 global pandemic was extremely lucrative for Amazon because we had to stay at home and quarantine, and many of us needed to order office supplies for our new workspaces. This crisis led to consumer deviation. This deviation led to profit for Amazon. In turn, the pandemic aligned with Amazon's profit goals. On the other hand, the pandemic also brought with it the deaths of one million Americans.

Malice

As you observe various systems, you may notice that their outcomes might not always align with the intentions of the humans who created these systems.

I've set aside a word to describe when these outcomes are harmful and the intent was to cause harm.

> **Malice** is the intention to do evil; ill will

Malice is often associated with hacking and hackers. This is because hacking typically involves deliberate breaking, and breaking can often be malicious. And if you were to immediately associate breaking with malice, you might lose sight of many of breaking's positive attributes.

You'll need to separate the constructs of malice and breaking in your mind. Those are two very different things.

Breaking a system can offer tremendous value—whether that system may be economic, societal, or technical. And breaking is fundamental to success in capitalism because breaking exposes new opportunities and resources that wouldn't otherwise be available. Without breaking, you lose vital opportunities to gain a competitive edge.

And breaking doesn't have to be malicious.

Animation

I have a special word to describe the process of bringing debris to life.

> **Animation** is the process of bring otherwise obsolete or dead resources into action; liveliness

Where there's destruction, there's debris. Where there's debris, there are new resources and newly exposed systems.

In my experience, there's a lot to be said for the practice of animating recent disasters' debris and the people who do this. Animating new life from debris draws on your ability to build and your ability to be resourceful. Rather than being able to rely on a shiny production cycle to offer money to cover the cost of building, animators subsidize the building process with debris instead of money. Animators perform advanced product development because the challenges of animating with debris likely yields unusual and uncommon resource for products that come from this. These constraints can be fascinating, and they can often yield clever solutions that later take the form of formal products! So new markets can often emerge from the ground of animation. Animating holistically can test even the most accomplished technologist.

I often look at animation as capitalism on expert mode.

If someone can identify a problem, design a solution, build the solution, and apply the solution to the problem using nothing more than harvested resources from previously broken systems, they're demonstrating expert-level mastery of their environment.

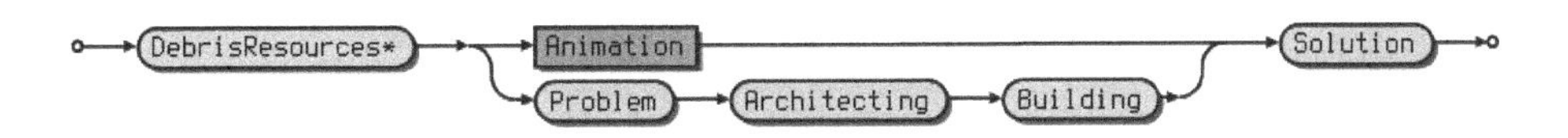

Identifying problems, architecting, and designing products are all essential steps to animation in the same way that they're essential to the production cycle and the building process. But animation has unique constraints that can challenge animators, such as developing products, architecting, engineering, marketing, and so on. You need a general understanding of how systems work to apply debris to solutions.

Applied Hacking

By drawing on the book's earlier chapters, you can apply breaking to common situations that tech workers like you find yourself in.

Sabotage (Animation)

Capitalism has consequences, and one of capitalism's consequences is that very good people can be very hurt.

It can be possible for otherwise good people to retaliate or try to harm.

> It's your first month at a new job in the tech industry. As you begin to venture beyond your immediate purview, you discover an alarming amount of debris in the company. You notice toxic behavior in the company and a general distaste for work. It seems that there are a group of workers who are very angry with the company.
>
> You soon discover there was an alarming situation that left a small group of employees angry with the company. It becomes apparent to you that the debris is a direct result of their actions against the company.

Their retaliation left a tremendous amount of debris.

Leadership was affected, policies were changed, and some workers even walked off the job. Engineers were assigned to manage systems they had never touched. Leaders were assigned to manage teams they had never met. This is one example of the type of catastrophic effects that can come about from breaking at a tech company.

Alongside this troubling discovery, you realize that you can't leave the company. You're stuck among the debris.

- How do you animate a system that will support your goals?
- How do you manage the overwhelming amount of debris?

Part of success in business is often very unfair, and often unrewarding. Managing debris, while often not "technically" the responsibility of a worker, can often times be looked down upon when it is missed.

The Recommendation

I'd suggest leveraging the situation for your career growth while addressing the debris.

This has the potential to further your personal goals while creating a more productive working environment for yourself and your colleagues. While the company will ultimately reap most of the benefits of this work, it can still be a viable tactic for the time being.

Amid the debris there's likely to be plenty of scared, hurt, or angry engineers who feel deceived by the company. By collaborating with them, you may be able to gain influence within the organization. With this influence comes authority and-ultimately-valuable career experience. Which creates the potential for a promotion or a raise.

Build something that you and your colleagues can be proud of.

But the product in this situation has little to do with the corporation's immediate needs. In this case, it has everything to do with escalating yourself and your colleagues who work on it.

This is a *growth* effort more than a *revenue* effort.

Traditional product management or engineering management might not be available to you in this situation. And an absence of funding and formal support for this will constrain your effort. But if you can build toward a common goal with limited resources in the wake of havoc, that's the epitome of animation.

In this situation, you understand that leaving the company won't be possible for a few months.

During that time, you might be able to take advantage of the havoc by working directly with leadership. While the organization is deviating from the norm, you'll have opportunities to fill the power vacuum.

Use the emergency to your advantage.

Even if you might not be able to get promoted, it can be worth pursuing a strong relationship with the leadership team even just to watch and learn. If you've made the decision to leave, there's little risk in pursuing a fast promotion or at least learning as much as possible.

Working directly with leaders to ask questions can help you identify the debris' state.

- Does the organization need direction?
- What could the company offer me if I were to step in and provide direction?
- Does it seem reasonable to try to influence the organization without the formal authority to do so?
- Could I get promoted if I were to bring structure to the broken organization?

This can be a good time to collaborate, especially if a promotion (or other upsides) seem available. Sharing your strategy with others and conveying to them that you also consider the organization's decision unacceptable could encourage them to trust you.

In a perfect world, you'd be able to quickly get promoted or—worst case—gain valuable experience from influencing the organization's direction before you look for a new job. Hyperfocusing on your career growth can make what would otherwise be an extremely unlucky career move one of the fastest escalations in your lifetime. So if you've already made the decision to leave, you have nothing to lose.

If you've made the decision to leave or if you at least want to improve the situation, you'll have some options. If nothing else, try to take what you can from the situation and leave on your terms when you can. Otherwise, brace for impact as you begin the slow work of rebuilding amid the debris.

Conclusion

Learn to embrace chaos.

Where there's chaos, there's opportunity. Where there's a problem, there's deviation. Where there's an emergency, there's disruption.

Destruction offers new opportunity and new growth. After every catastrophic forest fire comes a lush new undergrowth in the coming years.

Breaking, your ability to break, and breakers themselves are all relevant to your career. Developing a healthy relationship with the chaos can help you persevere through the cycles of building and breaking.

For every build cycle there's an equally relevant breaking cycle. Similar to a sine wave phasing in and out of harmony, cycles will tune themselves over time. In some cases, when a new project is created, another must be destroyed. For every wealthy project, another must be neglected. For every exciting innovation, a legacy system must rot.

This sway is similar to a pendulum swaying back and forth. Or the tides ebbing and flowing throughout the seasons. My observation has been that building and breaking occurs in cycles. Learning to identify the cycles and when various techniques can be leveraged is critical to gaining an advantage in the situation.

As a marginalized person, you can leverage your knowledge of these cycles to provide insight into which techniques will be more effective in a given situation.

In my opinion, building and breaking are a zero-sum relationship in organizations.

Understanding how breaking happens can improve your relationship with it. Breaking won't always be deliberate, and it certainly won't always be a viable tactic. And breaking oftentimes happens without explicit intervention. Like internet outages and natural disasters, breaking often happens without warning.

No matter what triggered a break-whether from an unexpected disaster or deliberate sabotage-the outcome is the same. After any breaking scenario, there'll probably be resources. There may be a lot of resources or there may be none. In many cases, there'll be resources that you can use in new ways.

This is where being a skilled builder and a wise breaker comes in to play. Learning to build innovations from the debris will be the difference in the future of the world's economies.

Aside from solar and wind power, our days of *raw* and *pure* natural resources are mostly over. Both in the natural world and in business. There are no longer *vast untouched forests* or *limitless oil reserves*. There are no longer excited university graduates or the limitless potential of cloud.

The same is true for technology, and a career path. The likelihood of blazing a truly new and pristine path is highly unlikely.

I can't help thinking about how adults are now reaching the workforce with a lifetime of insurmountable debt, unreasonable healthcare costs, and relatively few chances of gaining meaningful equity in their workplaces. Viewing these workers through the lens of the past is no longer be reasonable.

You need to realize that there's debris to begin with if you want to build new systems.

In some cases, the only resources you'll be able to consider will come from destruction instead of nature. Learning to build products from the broken carnage of yesterday will be the palette for the engineers of tomorrow.

Ultimately, deliberately breaking a system is a gamble, like rolling the dice in a game of Dungeons & Dragons. In some situations, the gamble will be worth it. In other situations, it won't.

Once havoc has ensued, the breaking has begun. Debris will follow, and you might be able to recover resources from the debris. Learning to envision the debris as resources takes special attention to detail.

Debris can also bring about deviations from the norm. Rules can change, organizations can be affected, and systems can be mutated.

These patterns are relevant to organizational structure, the economy, and computer science. Breaking a computer system could yield access to resources.

Hackers exploit computer systems by applying these resources toward their goals. You can also use the mentality of breaking to hack capitalism and to achieve your goals.

Chapter 8. Open Source

In my opinion, the most fascinating of all capitalist antipatterns in the tech industry is the concept of open-source projects and the collaborative communities that support them.

Despite your first impression, learning about open source software, and the communities that have made the projects thrive can be one of the most powerful thing a marginalized person can do when it comes to hacking the tech industry.

More importantly, loosely organized, grassroots, collaborative, free, and open projects can be directly responsible for tremendous profits for companies.

Despite capitalism's ruthlessness dominating the United States and broader global economies, open-source software has somehow been able to thrive. And in many cases, open-source software can often outperform even the most competitive environments.

There are extremely successful collaborative projects that have found success in challenging the fundamentals of competition in tech.

These projects have fostered monumental growth of the industry. These projects have brought about broader product development that wouldn't have otherwise been possible.

Many of these projects have been built, supported, and maintained completely for free.

> **Open Source** projects are composed of software, patterns, documentation, and reference architecture that the public can inspect, modify, enhance, or hinder.

Open source is a broad term, and it can apply to many styles of building and supporting technology. More importantly, *open source* is typically associated with software that's often released completely for free, independently of any corporation's product development.

Free Open Source Software or FOSS refers to software that is built and maintained in the public, freely licensed, and available for consumption for free.

The free and open-source software-development cycle is very similar to the traditional production cycle.

But the free and open-source software-development cycle is missing one important attribute: money. One production cycle is centered on profit, while the other is centered on the general good of humanity.

Proprietary software is closed-source software where the software manufacturer withholds the source code typically in order to protect recreation of a product; non-free software

Proprietary software is the opposite of (free) open-source software.

Companies heavily guard their methods for building, maintaining, distributing, and applying software.

A **Trade Secret** is an intellectually guarded and protected device, technique, pattern, or approach that is used by a company in its manufacturing process.

So I present the ultimate software conflict that is the banality of the tech industry.

On one end of the software spectrum, you find fiercely competitive proprietary software and tactics that are typically guarded with secrecy. On the other end of the software spectrum, you find generously collaborative open software and tactics that are given away for the good of humanity.

	Proprietary Software	Open Software
Behavioral	Competitive	Collaborative

Posture	Secretive (Closed)	Conspicuous (Open)
Cost Trend	Paid	Free
Motivation	Self-interest	Philanthropic
Goal	Profit	Altruism

Open-source software matters to capitalism because free and open-source software breaks and disrupts the industry.

Put plainly, free and open-source software is responsible for some of the greatest profit margins the industry has ever seen.

How does something that's given away for free create profit?

Open-source software is a necessary counterpart to proprietary software in the same way that collaboration is a counterpart to competition. When a system begins to swing too far to one side, you can disrupt the system by introducing an abundance of its antisystem. Observing and predicting this pendulum-like motion can be useful in micro- and macroeconomics.

To understand how you can apply these tactics, you must first understand what I think of as the subtle difference between collaboration and cooperation.

Cooperation

I think there's a subtle difference between cooperation and collaboration. These two economic strategies seem synonymous with each other, but I think that they differ in how each rationalizes their work as it affects their goals.

The chapter on collaboration defines collaboration as the process of working together to achieve a common goal.

I think that cooperation is a hybrid tactic that uses only the bare minimum of collaborative techniques to achieve an independent goal.

Collaboration is the antisystem to competition. And I think that cooperation is a hybrid of the two.

Cooperation is the process of working together to achieve an independent goal as a part of a broader effort.

In other words, I think that cooperation refers to operating independently, together. To "co-operate." And I think that cooperation is a hybrid technique that stems from competition and swings into collaboration just enough to accomplish a small goal. Here's how I think of them:

Competition	Cooperation	Collaboration
Independent goals	Independent goals through common effort (hybrid)	Common goals

You can see an example of this behavior in hardware manufacturers with software manufacturers.

Juli Clover at MacRumors notes that Taiwan Semiconductor Manufacturing Company (TSMC) builds all of Apple chips and has so for many years. Including the Apple M1 chips. [36] TSMC cooperates with other manufacturers including a recently announced joint innovation with Microsoft to accelerate silicon design on Azure. [37]

So the legendary and fiercely competitive Apple and Microsoft cooperate with the same silicon manufacturer while being at odds with each other economically.

Despite Apple and Microsoft's perpetual competition, which is woven together with cooperative hardware through TSMC, there's also a fully collaborative alternative.

Linux

Interestingly enough, Microsoft and Apple, despite how cooperative they may be with hardware manufacturers, have met a compelling adversary in the realm of computer operating systems.

Despite any interjections, even if only for a moment, from

sexually derogatory former MIT visiting scientists, Linux is (and always will be) simply a free and open source operating system.

Nothing more - Nothing less.

In my own words, *Linux* is the common name given to the Linux kernel in addition to the surrounding tools for most everyday kernel usage.

Linux is the largest open-source software project in history. [38] Linux and open-source software, including Android, is used on more cell phones and web servers in the tech industry than any proprietary operating system. [39] Linux and Unix-like operating systems make up roughly three quarters of public web servers [40], and Android makes up over half of handheld and mobile devices. This data suggests that despite its existence outside of competitive manufacturing processes, collaborative and cooperative software design still dominates many mobile and server markets. Or to put it simply, even the best products in the world face strong opponents from the free and open collaboration of computer scientists.

I'm a daily Linux user, and I've enjoyed the warm presence of knowing that a project built on altruism, collaboration, and teamwork can outperform even the fiercest of competitive products. In some way, Linux gives me hope for humanity because it shows that even at large scales, humans can do great things in the name of collaboration. I feel lucky that we're able to see something of this scale in our lifetime. I look forward to watching similar efforts develop as I grow older.

Linux is sustained with cooperation from the industry, and it's collaborative. Linux abstracts hardware to higher-level software that many of us use every day. Hardware manufacturers have incentives to contribute to Linux because the majority of public-facing web servers run Linux. The enterprise finds value in seamlessly operating on various hardware. Hardware manufacturers find value in exposing their hardware in standard ways. Linux distributes this work. Linux users, hardware manufacturers, professionals, enthusiasts, and practitioners have incentives to contribute to Linux. And even though each contribution may be motivated by independent goals, Linux is the intellectual glue that connects this modern computing stack.

Part of Linux's success comes from the way that it distributes work. Linux releases software on a regular cadence, and it has-relatively speaking-a low barrier to entry for new contributors. Having contributors work together in public to create economic value is what makes Linux the phenomenon that we see today.

Open Collaboration

Production cycles can happen independently of corporations, and they can often be more effective and more productive-while yielding better products-than their traditional corporate counterparts. And they also follow strikingly similar patterns to traditional production cycles.

Open Collaboration is an effort or system that relies on collaborative participants to subsidize an economic need; provide economic value with collaboration

I set aside the term *open collaboration* as a type of model that produces economic value without the capitalism's traditional incentives. So it's possible to contribute to society and stimulate an economy without working at a corporation. And collaboration outside of corporate environments can actually be more productive and create more value.

Open collaboration tries to produce value the same way that traditional product cycles do. The means of production can change, but software remains the outcome.

So open collaboration is to open-source software as the production cycle is to traditional products.

Open Collaboration Model

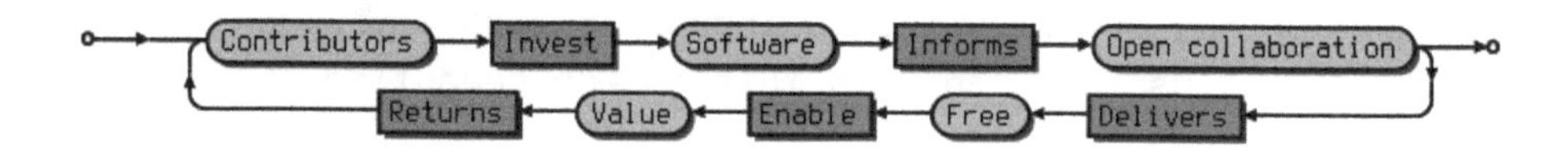

- Contributors develop software.
- Software affects the open-collaboration process.
- Open collaboration delivers a product for free.
- That value increases contributions.
- The cycle begins again.

The open-collaboration model is fascinating because it can create economic value that otherwise couldn't exist. Where there's new economic value, there will be new business opportunity!

> Open collaboration - which has brought the world Bitcoin, TEDx and Wikipedia - is likely to lead to new organizations that are not quite non-profits and not quite corporations.
>
> **- Sheen S. Levine of Columbia University and Michael J. Prietula of Emory University published in the journal Organization Science**

Collaboration and cooperation are viable approaches to making things. Collaborative models directly compete with traditional production cycles, and collaboration also supports products that otherwise wouldn't have been possible. Apple couldn't have made their ARM64-specific operating systems without the underlying cooperation from TSMC's chip manufacturing.

So to reiterate, collaborations can disrupt markets by creating products that otherwise wouldn't be possible.

Kubernetes

In the same way that Linux disrupted the operating-system market by fostering mass collaboration toward a common goal, Kubernetes similarly disrupted the cloud-computing market. Kubernetes is effectively distributed Linux built for container processes that were only possible because of new features in the Linux kernel. Some refer to this container-based distributed system as container orchestration. Personally, I just think of Kubernetes as distributed Linux along with YAML as the new-and less useful-Bash.

Kubernetes disrupted the cloud-infrastructure market. I've played an instrumental role in making this happen. Specifically I have created and maintained a number of open source infrastructure projects related to Kubernetes such as Cluster API, Kubicorn, and so on. My work at Heptio, VMware, Microsoft, Sysdig, and Twilio have all pushed myself, and the Kubernetes open source communities forward.

As of December 2021, Kubernetes is used by over five million developers. [41]

I expect this number to grow, and I think it's a strong sign of Kubernetes's adoption in the enterprise.

In my opinion, I do not believe that Kubernetes found success because of anything to do with its kernel abstraction or its ability to schedule containers. In my opinion, Kubernetes found success because of the way that it fostered collaboration at scale. Specifically the community that supports and maintains the project.

Kubernetes or, more importantly, the Kubernetes community has made drastic improvements to the open-collaboration model where Linux has fallen flat.

Linux has shown that collaboration is possible under capitalism. Kubernetes has shown that its contributors' experience is directly linked to economic value. So while Linux has shown that collaboration is a viable means of making things, Kubernetes has shown that the collaborative model can be commoditized.

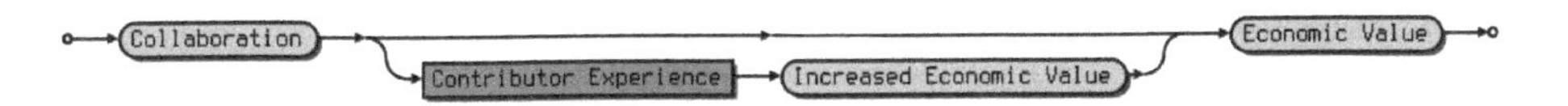

Specifically, the way that Kubernetes approached collaboration while prioritizing empathy was the disruption that the ruthlessness of capitalism needed to reset the enterprise. This was done using proven open-source tactics, with the most noticeable being the way that Kubernetes approached decision-making in public.

Decision-Making

Making a decision as a group can be powerful because all members of the group will inevitably feel ownership of the decision.

> **Group decision-making** is the ability to present a decision to a group, gain consensus, and communicate a clear path forward focused on a specific choice.

A certain amount of leadership is needed to identify a decision, drive consensus, and then communicate the decision to the group.

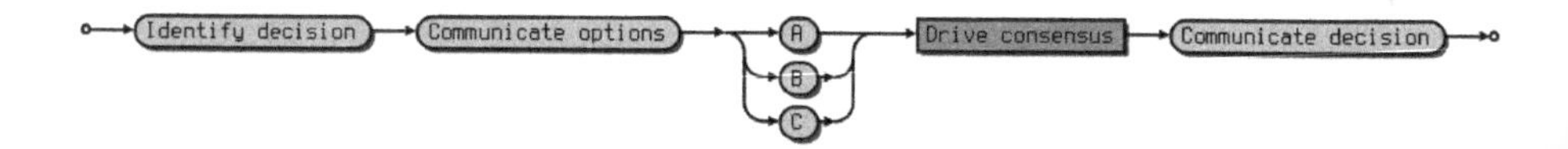

Kubernetes was able to standardize this process by creating the groups (known as special-interest groups) before decisions had to be made. A technical leader then only needed to identify the decision and work toward consensus. The group typically found prior art for communicating the decision, and the process quickly became a way for groups to easily and effectively make well-respected decisions. And as it turns out, driving consensus was often the most insignificant step in the process! Often, all that the groups needed to work toward consensus was an informal vote or even just some time for reasonable challenges.

Making decisions is a skill in its own right. But guiding a group of otherwise disparate technical contributors toward a decision requires specific tactics and strategies. Kubernetes is distinct from Linux in its ability to guide groups to well-understood and respected decisions. You can apply this egalitarian decision-making structure to business, computer science, and careers in tech.

So you can use this model to gain critical buy-in across a

corporation. You can use this model to set up a promotion for yourself or to alleviate road blocks and problematic personalities in your workplace. I suggest that anyone from a marginalized group heavily use this strategy to influence their organization. Putting a group behind a decision can be an easy way to mask the fact that the decision was made by someone who wouldn't have otherwise been respected.

Cooperative Extensibility

According to the definitions of cooperation and collaboration used in this book, neither Kubernetes nor Linux are "collaborative" projects.

I think that Kubernetes and Linux are cooperative projects.

Both Kubernetes and Linux are cohesive systems that are made up of smaller independent efforts that align with the cohesive vision. Each of the smaller efforts creates value for otherwise competitive contributors.

Software projects (like Kubernetes and Linux) and companies have a lot in common, particularly in the way that that software and companies both have to bootstrap themselves, and they both have build structure in places that have already been solved in the broader industry.

For example, almost every company at some point will need to dedicate resources to managing accounting, human resources, sales, production, and so on. In the same way, software projects also need to dedicate efforts to managing logging, runtime optimization, configuration management, modularity, and so on. C and C++ are notable for their need to reinvent the world for even the simplest use cases. Even the task of sending an HTTP request in C can require substantial amounts of boilerplate.

Software projects like Kubernetes and Linux have addressed this problem by having open-source efforts standardize a lot of what would've otherwise been considered unnecessary boilerplate. Companies, on the other hand, seem adamant about keeping their entire operating processes to themselves. Even if this means repeating that work.

Both Kubernetes and Linux acknowledge the need for modular cooperation, and they operate cooperatively. The software reflects this cooperative model in the form of Kubernetes's special-interest groups and Linux's subsystems and device trees.

For example Amazon might provide the ingress (a Kubernetes primitive) for the project, while Google might provide the egress (another Kubernetes primitive) for the project.

The project finds no reason to duplicate effort, so the work and scope of the modular components reflect this breakdown.

> **Cooperative Extensibility** is the deliberate design of breaking down work into modular components that can be fulfilled by cooperation of enabling independent efforts while adhering to a broader design; extensible through cooperation.

Kubernetes and Linux both leverage cooperative extensibility. These projects are extensible, and they allow for cooperative usage of the broader tool. These projects embrace this idea, and companies leverage this.

The tenant that the systems' designers adhere to is known as extensibility as the project becomes extensible.

> **Extensible** is the ability to extend, incorporate, or take advantage of in a generic way.

While open source certainly perfected extensibility, it took capitalism's hyperfocus on self-interest to perfectly apply extensibility to cooperation.

Projects like Kubernetes and Linux have shown that with thoughtful top-down architecture, you can build large cohesive distributed systems through cooperation. This approach is exactly what you need if you want to apply cooperation in your company. Because you can achieve independent goals while contributing to a broader system.

Architecture is what allows for this layered approach to cohesive systems through collaboration.

If you were to cooperate without a plan of how each extensible systems were to come together, you might find yourself with a dysfunctional collection of independent systems.

So cooperation without architecture is intrinsically risky. Architecture is the key to healthy cooperative extensibility.

Funding

Open-source cooperation and open-source collaboration both exist within capitalism. But money is such a fundamental component of capitalism that at some point every open-source project needs to address the critical question of funding various parts of the project.

Unfortunately, some capitalist theories put forward the idea that profit-driven companies have no obligations to society. Which means that companies don't think that they have any ethical obligations to cooperative software models. So it's completely legal and relatively common for companies to exploit the hard work of open-source efforts. Many believe, including me, that exploiting open-source projects without returning an equal amount of work toward the greater good of the project is morally unacceptable.

But exploitation of open-source software still happens.

The Log4Shell vulnerability known as CVE-2021-44228 reminded the industry of its exploitative relationship with open-source projects, particularly with regard to a lack of funding.

In December 2021, Filippo Valsorda, security lead on the Go team at Google, responded to the Log4Shell and Log4J events with an article about the importance of funding and investing in professional maintainers of open-source projects. [42]

The vulnerability was found in the Log4j codebase, which is owned and governed by the Apache Software Foundation. [43] The

Apache Software Foundation is a 501(c)3 Non-profit Charity EIN: 47-0825376. [44]

So the library is governed by a nonprofit, and it's used by the top companies in technology today. The association with profit is relevant. Companies like Microsoft, Amazon, and Google are profit motivated, while the Apache Software Foundation is explicitly not for profit. So in my mind, any company that uses the free library is effectively exploiting the library for profit.

The conflict in funding arises when companies that use the project don't finance those who maintain the project. This is particularly noticeable because the companies that use the project would be relatively unaffected by donating even a small amount of funding to the open-source efforts that they depend on.

Given the nature of self-interest, profit, capitalism's ruthlessness, and the licenses that open-source software is released under, it probably comes as no surprise that companies aren't legally responsible for funding any of this nonprofit work. The sad truth is that many open-source efforts continue on, underfunded and abused by large profit-driven companies.

The connection between open-source software and profit-motivated companies has always fascinated me. Particularly from a project quality standpoint. I remember growing up using Windows 95 and being completely astonished at how frustrating the user experience with Windows was. It was immediately obvious to me that Windows was a vehicle for profit, and Microsoft's goal for profit often came at the hostile expense of a user.

The user experience seemed to work well enough to get the user *close* to their desired outcome. In between success and my computer seemed to be a place for Microsoft to make a sale and for me, the consumer, to throw money at what appeared to be a pedantic problem.

I hated it instantly.

But Linux, an open-source alternative, seemed to simplify the interface without the bloat of profit-seeking motives. The interface was prioritized, and collaboration and cooperation seemed to dominate over Microsoft's competitive hunger for profit.

I loved it instantly.

Open-source efforts affect profit and funding. My experience has shown me that free and collaborative projects often deliver what I consider to be the best user experiences no matter how effectively companies might develop their products. It's not impossible for profit-focused products to have cohesive user experiences, but to me, that seems harder to do than under open and collaborative models.

For example, the iPhone was the first products in my adult life that seemed to actually work well. I was delighted and inspired to pay for it. Until that moment, I had never felt an urge to spend money on technology because collaboration seemed a better means to that end.

Transparency

To inspire cooperation, you'll need to communicate across the type of boundaries that capitalism has made difficult to bridge. Linux and Kubernetes have solved this by creating communication vehicles such as the Linux Kernel Mailing List [45] and the Kubernetes Slack instance [46].

In addition to those communication channels, there's also an open-source venue that fosters further cross-boundary collaboration: Kubernetes's open collaboration is hosted on GitHub. [47]

The ability to operate in a way that is conducive and helpful to other contributors is known as transparency.

> **Transparency** is operating in a way that optimizes on observation such that it is easy and convenient for others to see what actions are being performed.

GitHub's transparency has dramatically improved and incentivized the concept of working in public. Linux, for example, is often criticized for its extremely high barriers to entry and its cultural aggression. [48]

Kubernetes was able to show that prioritizing contributors' experiences with tools that support transparency can effectively engender cooperation with immediate upsides.

So by offering incentives for transparency, Kubernetes promotes cooperation.

In my opinion, Kubernetes engenders more cooperation than Linux.

Therefore, I believe that transparency can be directly linked to economic value with cooperative systems.

What this means to you in the tech industry is that working cooperatively and transparently can make your efforts more valuable!

For people from marginalized groups who are trying to outperform others, this can come into play when challenging organizational situations.

Transparency can create value.

Applied Hacking

Open-source software is a fascinating ecosystem. Particularly because of how open source, open collaboration, free software, and cooperation have been able to thrive and offer economic value in the otherwise ruthless system of competitive capitalism.

In situations where you need to challenge capitalism's constructs, you can draw on open-source software as an example of how to these efforts have achieved wonderful results in tech.

Security (cooperation)

Security is a unique compared to an organization's project work because security is rarely independent but rather woven through the other work. So security is often the most cooperative technical effort in an organization.

If someone needs infrastructure, they need to cooperate with security. If someone needs a database service, they need to cooperate with security. Someone needs an application stack, they need to cooperate with security. And so on.

Imagine that you have to lead a software project that will need to cooperate with a security team and some application teams. As the project leader, how might you use cooperative tactics from open-source projects to increase the project's value in the organization?

Breaking a project into layers that can easily be built on top of one another offers advantages from a software-design perspective and from a cooperation perspective. You can design effective software with clear interfaces, and you can also map the boundaries to cooperative efforts to allow for individual success.

Cooperation is achieving a greater goal as part of a broader effort. Consider structuring the software so that it's extensible and so that the various contributors can each be successful while still contributing to the broader project. But even the most extensible software designs won't always be able to satisfy security's need to evaluate every layer of the system.

The lessons of open-source software, cooperation, and transparent working habits can help you understand how you can encourage some constructs to increase the project's value.

The Recommendation

Encourage the application team and the security team to work transparently, and use a high-context communication style. This will make it easier for outsiders to understand context and effort, which will increase cooperation and visibility. This shift in working styles supports cooperation at the project level.

These changes in working styles might be uncomfortable for teams at first: Operating openly and transparently can feel risky and somewhat overwhelming. Teams might feel as if there's a small amount of safety in operating in a vacuum, but that safety rarely offers more value than transparency's rewards.

For example, if an application team had needed to ship an app and did so in isolation, the security team would need to evaluate the app-shipping process. Working transparently would encourage the team who's shipping the app to share the details of their process. By making the shipping process more visible, the team increases their situational awareness, and they also let security work cooperatively.

Transparency inspires cooperation, and cooperation creates value.

Structuring for Recognition (transparency)

Transparency creates value for the group that's being transparent and for anyone who's observing the group's actions. It's often said that if you build for a stranger, your future self will appreciate your efforts just as much.

There's another incentive if you want to exploit capitalism, especially for people from marginalized groups: When you operate transparently, you can structure your work in your favor. This tactic is relevant because it's inevitably harder for people from marginalized groups to get promoted and recognized than for people who aren't.

So when you're operating openly, take advantage of a platform that lets you tell a compelling story about your work. Advocating for your story will be easier if your story's artifacts are more visible!

Transparent communication is possibly the most important thing to focus on if you're looking for recognition.

> Imagine that you're working in a large organization, and you believe that you're due for a promotion. How would you go about illustrating your story? How would you gain recognition for your work?

Part of escalating toward the elite will involve gaining trust, and working closer to the inner circles. The ability to structure your work for recognition is an effective tactic in pushing someone closer to the elite.

One tactic that you can apply is to tell a detailed story of your actions. I suggest that all tech workers from marginalized groups keep journals of their work and include at least two items for each entry:

- A highly visible artifact of your work
- A highly visible relationship and communication trail

So if you want to operate transparently while you're seeking recognition, you need to find people and products for everything that you do. Of the two, relationships are by far the more important. It'll be in your best interest to have healthy, effective working relationships with each of the items that you use to support your story.

In fact, it can be more effective to focus on identifying people and products before you prioritize any outcomes otherwise! While it won't always be possible to do so, try to focus on the people and the visible outcomes before you worry about any of the mundane tasks.

Item	Relationship	Artifact

Last year, binary shipping.	Björn in infrastructure supports and uses my work.	The release impacted the organization, there was an email sent out, it unlocked Björn's team
Last year, cost analysis.	Disregarded by team's de-prioritization of cost analysis.	Designed and built system that calculated cost of our current application stack, was used to justify my promotion.
This year, cooperative application plugins.	Alice, Charlie, and Björn built plugins for the application stack.	Used cooperative extensibility to enable contributions to our work which enabled 3 subprojects to use plugins.

Look at this example journal of someone's work at a tech organization. Notice how they called out specific names and relationships. These names and relationships are relevant because they validate your work. And notice how there's an item in the journal that challenges the priorities of a team. In some situations, it can be in your best interest to focus on relationships and outcomes more than less visible busy work.

Once you decide to pursue a promotion, this journal will be what you'll use to justify your work. Each name should strongly support your work, and each item should be relatively easy to research.

Working transparently and diligently can open the door to high recognition for your work.

Conclusion

To reiterate, I think of cooperation as a hybrid strategy that sits neatly between collaboration and competition.

The relevance of open source is its ability to disprove the ideology that competition is the only means of success for distinguished impact to the economy. Understanding that cooperation and collaboration can be an effective means of delivering value can be useful to a marginalized person in the tech industry. In my experience collaboration, teamwork, and cooperation are viable ways for marginalized people to outperform their competitors.

Open source is a striking instance of specific collaborative constructs at scale. There is a lifetime of experience, stories, people, and demonstrable success in open source.

The concept of cooperation gives you the extensibility, and freedom, to effectively build projects at scale, such as Linux and Kubernetes.

Open collaboration lets you work toward a common goal. You can use open collaboration to cooperatively work toward goals too.

Regardless of your intended outcome, you'll need architecture if you want to create economic value.

Making decisions as a group is another tactic that you can apply if cooperation is your goal.

Funding open-source projects will inevitably be a problem as long as capitalism continues subscribing to the belief that companies have no obligations to society.

Understanding the economic effects of open source can help you gauge when you can apply various strategies. And open source can inspire transparent working habits. Strategically working transparently can be effective.

In addition to these tactics, such as group decision-making, transparent working, and cooperative extensibility, there's also a much broader concept that can be an extremely effective tool in hacking capitalism: influence.

[36] https://www.macrumors.com/guide/m1

[37] https://azure.microsoft.com/en-us/blog/microsoft-and-tsmc-announce-joint-innovation-lab-to-accelerate-silicon-design-on-azure/

[38] History of Linux, https://en.wikipedia.org/wiki/History_of_Linux

[39] Usage share of operating systems, https://en.wikipedia.org/wiki/Usage_share_of_operating_systems

[40] Usage Statistics of Operating Systems for Websites W3Techs, https://w3techs.com/technologies/overview/operating_system

[41] New SlashData report: 5.6 million developers use Kubernetes, an increase of 67% over one year, https://www.cncf.io/blog/2021/12/20/new-slashdata-report-5-6-million-developers-use-kubernetes-an-increase-of-67-over-one-year/

[42] Professional Maintainers: A wake-up call, https://words.filippo.io/professional-maintainers/

[43] https://logging.apache.org/log4j/2.x/

[44] Apache Software Foundation, https://projects.propublica.org/nonprofits/organizations/470825376

[45] The Linux Kernel Mailing List, https://lkml.org/

[46] Join Kubernetes on Slack, https://slack.k8s.io/

[47] Production-Grade Container Scheduling and Management, https://github.com/kubernetes/kubernetes

[48] The Art of Communicating with LKML,https://www.labbott.name/blog/2015/10/02/the-art-of-communicating-with-lkml/

Chapter 9. Influence

If there were a single word that I wish that I had paid more attention to earlier in my career, that word would be *influence*.

> **Influence** is the capacity to have an effect on the character, development, or behavior of others.

Influence is a tool that you can wield and apply to situations. It's a skill that you can develop, and the more that you learn to wield it, the more it'll be available to you.

Influence can reinforce and multiply the effects of all the lessons in this book.

For example, it's easier to engage large groups of folks toward working collaboratively if you can effectively influence them. So the better you are at influencing, the better you can harness the many benefits of collaboration.

Influence matters because influence is where you'll derive your impact and your power. Authority is something that can be theoretically given or awarded within an organization, but just because someone has a high-ranking title, that doesn't always mean that they can influence a group of people.

Typically, influence comes first, and then authority and title follow. Or at least that's the way that it's supposed to work.

It's no secret that authority and title are harder to achieve for people from marginalized groups. But influence remains a viable tactic that can often increase your chances of gaining higher authority and title. You can use influence for many things, and it isn't necessarily the only way to grow in title or authority.

Your ability to influence can be the difference between an introductory-level position and an executive-level position in a tech company. If you plan to escalate toward the elite in tech, you're going to want to be a champion influencer.

Influence—at its core—is an interpersonal skill, meaning that there's no exact formula for how to build influence with someone. So every situation will be different, and every character in the story will bring their own history and backstory. You'll need to assess each situation and apply tactics based on what you observe.

Begin by listening and observing the situation. And after you listen and deeply consider the situation, opportunities will begin to present themselves.

While observing a situation, you can pick up on many sentiments. Among the sentiments that you discover, some will be worth reinforcing, while others will be worth ignoring. Find the sentiments that align with your goals and reinforce those. And ignore the sentiments that conflict with your goals.

While you're using positive reinforcement to influence, you can also consider other leadership tactics. Inspiring others to work toward goals is a substantial part of leadership. When you inspire others, don't exploit them or harm them. Many times, inspiration can come in the form of ideas or helpful suggestions.

> Influence is giving your ideas away to others. If you have a good idea, just give it to someone else and let them run with it.
>
> — Bryan Liles, Principal Engineer

In other words, influence can be thought of as simply giving your ideas away.

Ideas

The tech industry loves a good idea, as does capitalism.

> Idea is a thought, sentiment, or suggestion to satisfy an anticipated outcome.

The tech industry is full of examples where profound technological ideas have shaped the economies of the world. But capitalism is built on competition, which might give you the impression that some amount of secrecy around profound ideas can help you sustain a competitive edge. Trade secrets are effectively heavily guarded ideas. These ideas, from a legal perspective, become a type of property that a company can claim ownership over.

> **Intellectual Property** is an intangible property that one can claim the rights over; a valuable idea with a concept of ownership.

So if a capitalist entity were to be interested in claiming intellectual-property rights over an idea, and if they were to file for a patent or a trademark, the idea could be protected by law. This creates a sense of secrecy and rivalry, and a defensive intellectual posture. This tendency to conceal ideas is a consequence of competition in capitalism. But concealing ideas is counterproductive to your ability to influence.

So while concealing ideas can appear to be helpful toward an organization's goals, it can be damaging to those in the midst of the situation.

This contrast is paradoxical.

- Capitalism tells us to keep our ideas a secret.
- Influence tells us to give our ideas away.

> If you're lucky enough to have a good idea, you're smart enough to know whether to give it away or keep it a secret.

Understanding that there are multiple ways to think about an idea-with repeatable outcomes-is a substantial part of learning how to influence in the tech industry. While there's tremendous value in bringing someone into an inner circle, such as the elite, there's also tremendous risk is creating such circles because their impact and potential are limited.

Personally, I take a somewhat reckless absolutist approach. I always give my ideas away, regardless of their perceived value.

There are drawbacks to this approach because I've likely lost out on some money-making opportunities in my career. But I've been able to live as a collaborative influencer, and that's more important to me than money.

Conceal Ideas	Divulge Ideas
It can be useful to conceal ideas, even temporarily if the outcomes or consequences is unknown or difficult to predict.	Divulge ideas when the outcome is desirable, and the means of achieving the outcome is irrelevant.

Adoption

Nothing validates and confirms an idea more than seeing the idea adopted by others.

> **Adoption** is assuming responsibility, or ownership of an external idea as one's own.

The social element and general hype that comes with adoption is extremely real (and somewhat deceptive). Personally, I despise how much validation hype can impose in large part because that sort of validation is the epitome of an appeal to popularity fallacy.

Ideas gain validation the more that they're perceived to be embraced and taken advantage of. This is a useful concept, especially for leaders and engineers working in tech.

Adopting ideas is an easy way for people to help others. Someone can support another person's goals of influencing an organization just by supporting and adopting their idea. This means that the traditional bottom of the tech industry can influence entire organizations or corporate cultures just by collaborating or working as an organized team.

And validating an idea through adoption can help to improve the idea by putting it through its paces. A large amount of adoption often brings with it a greater resiliency and rigidity to ideas. So the more that ideas are used, the more established and trusted they tend to become.

Well established describes the sentiment of trust that is experienced as ideas are exercised over time; battle tested.

This comes into play as you weaponize ideas toward your goals and self-interests. And since giving an idea away is one way that you can influence a group of people, you can also validate the idea by increasing adoption.

The more adoption an idea has, the stronger and more compelling it becomes. Ultimately, peers, colleagues, bosses, and other technical professionals can all be persuaded by adoption.

If you're from a marginalized group, you'll unfortunately need to draw upon tactics like adoption to compete at the same level as your peers.

Get good at sharing your ideas with others. Encourage them to celebrate your combined victories. Ultimately, using adoption to build hype is a fallacy. But it's a fallacy that can be surprisingly effective toward supporting your goals.

Presentation

Since ideas and adoption can validate your efforts, and since you want to influence a group a people, it's worth understanding the value of presentation.

Presentation is the task of preparing and delivering information in a meaningful, useful, and digestible way for others.

Presenting information can be exciting! There are many techniques to communicate ideas.

Whether you're presenting information in an informal meeting with your colleagues or presenting on television to the world, the process of delivering information to an audience remains the same. So if you want to be good at influencing others and have your ideas adopted, you'll need to become adept at communicating your ideas and delivering them to groups.

You need to know how to present because that's how you can communicate to a group. Typically, the person who's presenting information is also the person who's crafting the message. So if you're skilled at delivering information, you can often have a substantial effect on the message.

> Those that communicate, are those that influence the message.

This nuance is meaningful when giving large formal presentations, such as delivering updates to an organization. For people from marginalized groups, this tactic is even more meaningful for informal conversations. The ones that the organization doesn't sponsor. Any grassroots effort will have the same obstacles as a formal effort-and more. So you'll have to do the same tasks as the people who you're trying to outperform, but you'll have to do better. This includes presenting and communicating.

My preferred method of presenting is similar to a breadth-first search algorithm, if you might be familiar with that. I first build a tree of topics that I'd like to cover, and I briefly introduce each child topic in the first layer. Then, after talking about the first layer's topics, I circle back and dive deeper into each of the child topics' child topics. It's a technique that works well for communicating complex ideas.

1. First topic	2. Second topic	3. Third topic
1. First topic expanded	1. First topic expanded	1. First topic expanded
2. Second topic expanded	2. Second topic expanded	2. Second topic expanded

3. Third topic expanded	3. Third topic expanded	3. Third topic expanded
1. First topic summary	2. Second topic summary	3. Third topic summary

In this example, there are three nodes, and I've mapped each node to a topic. To communicate the broad strokes, I first introduce each of the three nodes. After introducing each of them, I revisit them in order and provide more detail. I elaborate on each node, and then I revisit the higher-order nodes.

For example, if I were to give a talk on how to influence people, I'd first explain the high-level system (influence) and how it's composed of smaller systems (ideas, adoption, and presentation). I'd then elaborate on the smaller systems to add more clarity. Then I'd revisit the broader topic of influence, and I'd connect the subsystems together.

To influence someone, you need to understand the importance of your ideas, how to get them adopted, and how to communicate the process.

First give your ideas away. Your ideas will become someone else's idea. Collaborate and share your ideas. Encourage the good parts and ignore the rest.

Next, encourage and reinforce adoption. If others begin to use your idea, showcase that adoption. Create incentives for people to adopt your idea.

Finally, communicate this process well. Present the information and the overview of the effort in a digestible way for others to see. It should be easy for others to see how well you can influence others.

You can increase your influence by finding good ideas, giving them away, encouraging adoption, and presenting your work.

As it turns out, this can be a surprisingly effective way to communicate complex ideas.

> As a note, I use this technique to structure the chapters in this book. The beginning sections touch on each of the subsections. Then I expand on each subsection. And then I revisit everything again.

Listening

To influence someone, you first have to understand and empathize with them.

To understand someone, you must consciously absorb their experiences. I draw a difference between *listening* and *understanding*. Listening is one of the techniques that you can use to understand others. Whether you reach an understanding through listening or other means, as long as you get to an understanding is what matters.

> **Understanding** is to be sympathetically aware of other's experience; to comprehend.

The word listening can often be as a false synonym for understanding. In this text, I use the word understanding directly.

Understanding someone lets you take their perspectives into consideration. You'll need this skill especially if working collaboratively or cooperatively is going to be a part of your strategy to outperform the elite. So if you aren't considering others' experiences, you won't be able to work collegiately.

You can use collaboration to outperform competitive cultures!

If you want to give your ideas away, help them gain adoption, and otherwise influence a group, you'll need to understand what's important to the group. By taking the time to truly offer sympathetic consideration, you can understand the needs of others. Once you understand their needs, you'll have a chance to align their needs with your goals.

This relationship is what I think of as cooperation.

The ability to cooperate begins with understanding.

When in doubt, shut up and listen.

Broadcasting

Being a part of leadership means repeating yourself. A lot.

It will also mean being deliberate about how, where, when, and with who you share your message.

In the same way that authors of news headlines and thoughtful tweets put an effort into effectively delivering messages with limited language, you as a leader will also need to deliver memorable and easy-to-understand messages. You're going to have a limited number of characters to reach your audience, and you'll need to broadcast effectively.

Broadcasting is the transmission of digestible information at scale.

There's an art to broadcasting a message, especially in tech. You've probably been on the receiving end of broadcasting before. Tech companies also have a history of broadcasting unofficial messages.

My advice to anyone starting to broadcast messages is to start small, and keep it simple.

Begin broadcasting any message with a small group of trusted colleagues who are likely to go along with your message. Grow the message, and your influence from there. Ask your colleagues to also broadcast the message on their channels.

The ability to communicate complex ideas will be a large part of your job as an influencer. The ability to communicate complex ideas quickly and easily, is what separates good influencers from great influencers.

For example, Google has successfully broadcasted the simple message "Don't be evil," but it hasn't necessarily kept up its end of the bargain, such as by firing employees who were trying to organize a union. [49] Microsoft similarly internally has "Embrace, extend, extinguish."

These sound bites aren't official branding, but they've been broadcasted enough that they're effective in delivering their messages. Google was able to communicate a complex idea quickly. This is desired.

Broadcasting is an important part of influencing large groups of people. For example, if you may have read through the earlier lessons and you came to realize that collaboration could be an effective tactic for you, you might try broadcasting to try to influence a large group of people toward collaboration. Collaboration can have consequences, but it can also be effective. You can use tools like broadcasting to reinforce messages to privilege-escalate to the top of the industry.

So you're going to need to repeat yourself at scale. You're going to have to craft your language and deliver it across many channels.

And in the same way that engineers might practice writing different programming languages, leaders might need to practice broadcasting technical messages in different situations.

Be ready to repeat yourself. Be ready to take complex ideas, and simplify them. Be ready to start small, and grow from there.

Empathy

Empathy is a superpower within the tech industry. Empathy can be highly effective toward influencing others.

I often feel guilty about drawing on empathy to influence.

On one hand, empathy is the essence of the human condition. Humans are social creatures, and empathy is something that all of us crave during our short lives on this planet.

On the other hand, using empathy to affect or change behavior might come across as manipulative. Almost a violation of the sacred bond.

> **Empathy** is the ability to understand and share the experience of another.

The ability to empathize in tech is a superpower. The elite typically detach themselves from others and deliberately withhold empathy from others. Capitalism seems to have a way of encouraging a distaste for empathy, especially among those who grow closer to the capital. Capitalism tends to favor competitive personalities. These personalities often view kindness and empathy as forms of weakness.

But empathy is critical to leadership. And leadership is critical to cracking the code of the tech industry.

Showing empathy to others is an effective way to influence them and to improve existing plans and designs. Understanding other people's external experiences can lead to thoughtful and resilient designs.

Advocacy

Influencing others is about creating a common belief in an idea. You may need to be tactful about which ideas you suggest. The process of selecting an idea and fostering a belief in the idea is the essence of influence.

> **Advocacy** is public support and endorsement of a particular cause, platform, effort, or idea.

The process of gaining buy-in or developing a common mindshare around an idea is known as advocacy.

> **Mindshare** is a shared vision or belief in the minds of a group of individuals; public awareness.

Advocacy is important to success in capitalism because many

ideas will require not only execution but also advocates for them to exist in the first place.

So no matter what project you're working on or the level that you're trying to influence, you need to be able to convince others that your approach to solving a problem is viable.

You can reinforce advocacy with other techniques such as giving away your ideas, broadcasting them, and fostering their adoption.

For instance, many tech companies will employ advocates specifically for this.

> A **Developer Advocate** is someone who advocates for developer experience with a specific tool, project, or product.

Whether advocacy is your full-time job or just a tool that you occasionally use at the office, advocacy matters. You'll need to be able to advocate for your ideas in tech.

In fact, one of the quickest ways for someone from a marginalized group to gain value in an organization is to get their ideas widely adopted. In my experience, getting your ideas adopted is one of the few ways to break the invisible glass ceiling faced by people from marginalized groups. So if your ideas are perceived to be valuable, you can count on the elite to try to exploit them for profit. Advocacy is an extremely effective way to help others see the value in your ideas and to escalate yourself to the inner circles of the elite.

Be warned with taking a position as a full time advocate. Remember that the primary goal of an organization within capitalism is to seek revenue. During economic uncertainty (such as the recession of 2020) it can be harder for organizations to justify paid altruism. During these phases of low revenue an advocate's job is likely to be diminished to technical marketing as it has a tighter and more demonstrable return on investment.

In capitalism there is no such thing as paid altruism.

Social Media

Social media is a fascinating layer of influence because it exists at the broader economic level.

Social Media is an internet-based form of communication that allow users to engage, influence, and share content.

Social media is a layer of communication, advocacy, and industry influence that spans companies, with Twitter being the most common in the tech industry.

Social media matters because it can house discussions that exist above the corporate level. For example, in previous chapters, I shared my perspective that companies that exist under America's system of capitalism have no ethical obligations to society. At best, companies might hold themselves to an internal set of standards or to language like Google's "Don't be evil" standard.

Because social media spans companies, whenever a company such as Google does something that society deems evil, social media tends to be the venue that houses the backlash.

Because social media exists at a macroeconomic level, it can be a strong medium for challenging companies' behavior.

So just because I don't think that companies have an ethical obligation to society, that doesn't mean that society won't retaliate against companies, which can then affect their profits.

Under capitalism, companies crave profits, and social-media campaigns are a proven way to affect those profits. I look at a well-orchestrated social-media campaign as a collaborative sanction that society can impose on bad actors. This ability to sanction companies for behaving unethically is one of the few tools that we have for combatting their behavior under capitalism.

You can also use social media to influence at the company level.

For example, because Kubernetes is widely adopted across many companies, you can cite its wide adoption to influence other companies to adopt Kubernetes too.

Ultimately, social media is your main artery for economic influence. If you plan to go big in tech, social media is going to be where you exercise your influence.

Applied Hacking

The myth of meritocracy under capitalism is especially widely held among people with privilege.

The idea that you just need to work hard to be rewarded isn't viable for anyone who isn't straight, white, and male. So people from marginalized groups need to take that reward, acknowledgement, and profit by force. These things are never given away under capitalism, especially not to anyone from marginalized groups.

Influence is a tool that many will claim is a viable way to grow in your career. But there's nuance in how you apply influence. Traditionally, you would influence others to inspire work and mindshare across a group on behalf. But in this section, I'll go over how you can apply influence toward your goals.

By learning how to influence on your terms, you can learn

perhaps an even more valuable skill, which is being able to tell when your influence is effective. You want to learn how to advocate for your own goals before you advocate for another.

I'm a proponent of the idea that prioritizing your self-interest is critical to hacking capitalism. In the same way that airplanes' emergency procedures encourage passengers to put on their own masks before assisting others, I encourage readers to satisfy their needs first before working on behalf of an organization.

> Pay yourself first.

Learn how to influence the organization to serve your needs before you learn how to influence an organization to serve their needs. As it turns out, you can achieve both if you first focus on yourself.

Attrition

Imagine that you're working at a large tech company. Many people are leaving the company because of external factors, poor leadership, perpetual ambiguity, confusion and organizational dysfunction.

> **Attrition** is the departure of employees from an organization.

There quickly becomes a noticeable attrition problem. As the attrition grows, it becomes clear that the company's leadership needs help influencing the organization toward a more sustainable working environment.

How do you influence the organization toward a productive and enjoyable working environment while first prioritizing your own needs?

Recommendation

My recommendation is that you position yourself as a trusted thought leader for the organization. Begin to influence the organizations toward a hopeful future. Be the voice of hope in the company.

Make use of tools such adoption and broadcasting not necessarily to influence your colleagues toward productivity-but to influence the rest of the organization to recognize your ability to lead. So if you broadcast a message, let the message establish that you're a leader offering hope. If you're successful in clearly broadcasting your message, there can be little doubt that you'll come out ahead. You can to position yourself not as a bottleneck but as a champion. And that without your leadership, the hope would begin to fade and the attrition would further develop.

Now, the consequence of this behavior is that if you decide to leave the company, the attrition is likely to rekindle. On one hand, this is a case of history repeating itself; on the other hand, this can be a chance for another thought leader to emerge.

If you're from a marginalized group and if you want to be awarded even the most baseline of merit, you'll need to be able to broadcast messages that are so clear that they'll be impossible to challenge. So you'll have to overachieve to gain the same rewards as your peers who have greater privilege. Influence is a proven way to effectively do this.

Conclusion

Influence matters because it's the main currency in the tech industry.

So much so that many organizations, projects, and companies have influence-based cultures. Which means that senior and executive titles comes from the ability to influence others well. And if someone in the tech industry can influence without authority, they can operate at whatever level of the company they chose. If your goal is to escalate yourself to the inner elite circles of the tech industry, influence is going to be how you'll get there faster than your peers. A quick way to influence someone or a group of people is to give them your ideas. In spite of capitalism's perpetual pressure to conceal and guard ideas in hopes of greater profits, it can be effective to reject that pressure for a moment and give your ideas away in the hopes of inspiring collaboration.

Giving your ideas away is a good thing because that can kick-start the building process for others.

The process of getting others to accept your ideas away is known as adoption. Once an idea has been adopted, it will hopefully change, improve, and grow independently of the author.

As your idea comes to fruition, you'll need to advocate for the idea in the hopes of further influence and adoption. The skill of presenting an idea effectively is known as presentation. This book shares a detailed example of how you can present complex ideas in a breadth-first approach. (First, describe each topic at a high level. Then circle back and drill into each topic.)

Perhaps an even simpler way of communicating is to break your message into two questions:

- What is it?
- Why does it matter?

Which, if you review this book, you'll notice that every section loosely follows this formula of first defining what something is and then why it matters.

To be empathetic, you must first listen to others. Empathy is a proven way to gain trust and escalate to an organization's the inner circles. Listening is a proven way to build empathy.

Listen more.

Advocating is another way to communicating ideas. This comes in the form of interpersonal skills, conversational skills, and communication skills. Advocacy is different from defending an idea or, worse, playing devil's advocate. Advocacy is endorsement, an authentic belief in something. If a belief is genuine, encouraging the spread of the idea should come naturally.

Finally, social media can be as toxic, damaging, and harmful as it is effective. I and other notable social-media advocates have been known to take extended breaks from social media and even break down at times from social media's mental-health consequences. But you can also use social media combat the ruthlessness of capitalism and to influence others. My direct advice would be to be tactful with social media. The moment that social becomes an escape, a form of comfort, a quick hit of dopamine, or a surrogate therapist, that can be extremely dangerous.

Treat social media the same way that you treat work. Have a plan, know what you want out of it, and use it to get what you're after.

Ultimately, learning to influence others in tech can take a lifetime of work. It can be very personal, and oftentimes it'll be connected to your personal journey in the industry. Certain skills, examples, pieces of language, and experiences can all contribute to your ability to influence.

Influence is—within itself—a skill.

A skill that's worth developing.

[49] Google Fired Employees for Union Activity, Says US Agency" BBC News, December 3, 2020, https://www.bbc.com/news/technology-55173063.

♻ Chapter 10. Sustainability

One of my good friends often reminds me that careers are fantastically long.

So because you'll likely be working in your career for decades on end, any given action is only viable toward accomplishing your goals if it's sustainable. And we all need to play the long game.

> **Sustainability** is the ability to maintain an effort at a current rate, level, efficiency, or effectiveness.

You'll need to pay great attention to make sure that the tactics that you choose to use from this book will be available time and time again without the risk of those actions depleting your vital resources.

Actions include things like choosing when to wake up for work in the morning or multibillion-dollar organizations delivering products year over year. No matter what you're doing, you'll likely need to sustain your efforts for years on end.

Each action requires resources, so your ability to sustain an action depends on your ability to replenish those resources. This concept particularly comes into play with for-profit systems and operational costs. (It appears that capitalism takes the term human resources a little too seriously, and it likes to think that humans are part of a zero-sum system.)

While sustainability may seem like a simple concept, there are many contributing factors that you can evaluate to predict a system's sustainability.

 Glaciers

You can draw many useful metaphors of economic sustainability from glaciers.

> A **Glacier** is a persistent body of ice that will move or "flow" under its own weight. Often found on steep inclines at higher elevation.

On a geological scale, a glacier may exist only briefly. But a glacier will often persist over many human lifetimes. And if you observe a glacier year after year, you can start to see trends. As the Earth revolves around the sun and we experiences seasons, a glacier has a chance to grow in the winter and melt in the summer.

(An upshot of this is that glaciers are an ideal indicator for the broader health of the planet because scientists can take yearly measurements that reveal geological trends.)

For a glacier to sustain itself, it needs to replenish itself faster than it depletes itself.

> **Accumulation** is the rate at which a glacier replenishes itself with snowfall or other precipitation.

There's a relationship between the forces that replenish glaciers and those that deteriorate glaciers.

As you exist in the tech industry, you can think of yourself as a glacier.

There will be factors that support your ability to grow and expand in size. And there will also be factors that wear on you and those that cause you to burn resources or deplete them over time.

At times, the size of your influence or reach can become counterproductive, much like a glacier.

There are geological moments when the sheer size of a glacier is so large that its mass causes it to fall faster into lower elevations and higher temperatures, resulting in the glacier receding faster than it can replenish. Glaciers can also have broader swings of more massive generations and more minuscule generations that outlive the yearly melt cycle.

In the tech industry, you'll need to be aware of your ability to replenish yourself. As a leader, you'll need to be aware of the organization's ability to replenish itself.

The tech industry loves to burn resources because the tech industry is a part of capitalism. Workers in capitalistic environments are notoriously never paid their worth, resulting in capitalism being a textbook example of a system that diminishes its own resources.

If you were a glacier, you'd begin your career in a state of receding faster than you can replenish.

Burnout

You need to stay healthy and mentally active if you want a sustainable a career in tech.

In the tech industry, there are many factors that can stretch your mental health to a critical point. Oftentimes the tech industry will take more and more emotional and mental reserves without replenishing them.

Getting to the point where you're hitting the red line is unfortunately common. This is a direct result of the worker extortion that the tech industry is founded on. This is known as *burnout*.

Burnout is an exhausted mental state caused from consuming more resources than are available; debilitating stress without aid.

Burnout is caused by overexerting someone without providing the tools, resources, and support to counteract that exertion.

In other words, burnout is caused by a *do more with less* mentality.

Capitalism is founded on competition, and overexerting yourself is often rewarded because that can offer a competitive advantage. But as the number of competitors increases, that will only increase the need to overexert yourself to maintain your competitive edge.

You can sometimes offset the need to overexert yourself with automation. (I often ask myself how many jobs I've automated away in my lifetime just to make myself worth more than my peers.)

Perhaps the reason that the tech industry has flourished in the United States is because of its relentless obsession with competition. In other countries, perhaps there isn't as much reward for using technologies as competitive tools. Or perhaps tech's exploitive nature isn't as viable in countries that have implemented worker protections and viable social safety nets.

No matter what tools you use to compete, all labor comes at a cost. If you don't pay special attention to replenish the resources that you need, and if your environment becomes unsustainable, you won't be able to continue.

☻ Smiling

It can be hard to give concrete advice about mental health. Many articles and books suggest superficial techniques such as diet or exercise for better mental health. While these things can certainly be effective for some, telling someone to transition to a plant-based diet isn't necessarily going to help them to sustain an onslaught of abuse from the tech industry.

You need to identify factors that you can use to measure your internal state. So what are some things in your daily life that might offer insights into the state of your mental health?

> I suggest starting to measure your smiles per day.

Smiling indicates joy and a feeling of safety and peace. I think that smiling can be a strong indicator of a healthy internal state. Learn to identify what a smile feels like. Learn to identify which people and situations you find yourself smiling around. Prioritize these situations, and prioritize these feelings.

Personally, I find myself smiling around people who I've developed trust with. My partner, my puppy, my good colleagues at the office, and so on. I hold these situations to be just as important as a meeting with an executive. I give these situations special attention on my calendar. I'll quite literally schedule time to relax and have fun—just to make sure that I get in a certain number of smiles per day.

While smiling may not be the only metric that you can use here, I think it's a good starting point. There are other metrics, such as blood pressure, a good night's sleep, appetite, social engagement, personal hygiene, self-respect, and so on.

Ultimately, it doesn't necessarily matter whether what you're accomplishing is a smile or a laugh or just a feeling of peace and tranquility. The takeaway is that you should feel something other than the need to overexert yourself in capitalism. Find things that ground you and give you purpose in life.

🏃 Endurance

Smiling and burnout aren't a zero-sum game. You'll have to work toward the things that bring you joy. This is especially true under capitalism.

Smiling can require just as much work as existing under capitalism. In fact, in the US, it can feel almost impossible to smile unless you're getting something in return.

Capitalism likes to pretend that a smile is something that you get from buying things. So if you were to subscribe to that reasoning, smiling would be a privilege for those with disposable income.

You'll need to be able to endure this grueling economic system if you want to exploit capitalism.

Endurance is the ability to persist or sustain through a challenging situation over time.

Resources like sleep, food, and tools can support your work and ultimately support your happiness. So you need to harvest resources sustainably so that you can use them time and time again.

Endurance is more about your ability to recharge than it is about your ability to exert.

Endurance is measured by the rate that you can recharge to the point that you can once again exert your original effort. And by minimizing how much downtime you need to recharge, you can get more done.

This is relevant within capitalism because capitalism is notoriously a competitive race to the top. It's more effective to have a sustained pace that's slightly faster than your competition than it is to have an extremely fast pace that's short lived. So your overall progress is more relevant than your top speed.

Collaboration is the key to endurance.

Collaborating with others and focusing on your common goals is the key to making sure that you have the critical free time to recharge. Capitalism makes this hard because capitalism positions you in a competitive state by default.

Defying the pressure to be competitive can feel counterproductive, but that can ultimately be a more effective endurance strategy.

You might try to find yourself a group of like-minded hackers to partner with. Identify a common goal, and cover one another while others recharge. You can give one another the gift of a true break if a subset of the group can on take the brunt of the force while others safely recharge.

 Resource Allocation

You'll need to have a realistic view of the resources that you need to do each task so that you can map out how to sustain the task.

> **Resource Allocation** is the ability to map resources required to complete a task, with a specific interval of task performance.

Capitalism, specifically the production cycle, pretends that the world can run on money alone.

But a sustainable system also needs many other resources. Or to put it another way: Money doesn't come for free. People like you need to create value for companies so that companies can generate a profit.

If capitalism is fueled by money, and money is a byproduct of labor, then capitalism runs on labor.

Labor and—more importantly—time from workers like you. System can be made up of humans or computers—or a combination of both.

- Capitalism is an economic system.
- Kubernetes is a computer system.
- An engineering organization is a hybrid system
- and so on…

All systems require resources. And when a system depends on humans, there are associated resource costs.

Breaking a task into a single unit of completion is an effective way to project what resources it'll use so you can gauge its sustainability. So if you can identify either a project's timed cadence or a measurable point in the cycle, that'll make it easier for you to predict what resources it'll use.

For example, you can use a year as a yardstick to gauge work and labor. You can gain an understanding for how much time you need to recharge each year.

> European Union legislation mandates that all 27 member states must by law grant all employees a minimum of 4 weeks of paid vacation. [50]

The United States is notoriously horrific about offering recovery time (paid vacation). Without recovery time, sustainability may not be possible. So it's no surprise that the United States has one of the worst burnout and attrition problems in the world.

Using a single year to measure the work-versus-recovery ratio lets you see how much time you need to set aside for resource regeneration.

Systems need time to recover to remain sustainable. That includes computational resources, energy resources, labor, organizational structures, manufacturing resources, and so on.

By understanding the amount of resources needed to do a discrete task, you can project how many resources you'll need. And you can make similar projections for resource regeneration.

Capitalism likes to view regeneration requirements as operating costs.

Somewhere along the way we've lost track of the idea that operating costs are more than just money.

💵 Currency

Time, effort, energy, and focus are all resources that you as a technologist can spend.

As you grow and develop your skills, you'll inevitably find situations that will be wise to spend your energy on. You'll also probably find situations that would be foolish to focus on.

You'll need to gauge which situations have the biggest draw on your skills and energy so that you can spend your resources efficiently.

Resource Currency is the hypothetical units of energy that can be potentially spent on an effort.

Having autonomy over your currency won't always be possible. But advocating for your currency being spent wisely is always worth considering.

To remain sustainable from a resource perspective, you'll have to spend your currency wisely to the extent that you can. In some cases, it might even be possible for you to become so efficient at spending your currency that you'll be able to spend less time (energy) than the time (energy) that you get in return.

Sustainable Design

There are a lifetime of systems and relationships that we observe during our short time on this planet.

As you observe systems, you observe their nature, their inputs, and their outputs.

Sustainable Design is the practice of ensuring that the outcomes of a particular system contribute to the resources required to execute the system.

You can—with enough attention to detail—design systems such that you can recycle the outputs of one system and use them as inputs in your system. When the byproduct of one system might not directly feed back into itself, you can often use that as a resource or input for another system.

An example that comes to mind in tech is that because tech pays more than many other industries (especially for technologists without college degrees), technologists can sometimes take breaks between jobs. In this case, you can use the output of the first job—money—as an input for a break that you can use to satisfy a longer-term investment in yourself. As long as you structure your broader path with these breaks in mind, you can sustain a well-executed career.

Protection

As long as capitalism exists, there will be tremendous pressure to overexert ourselves. Capitalism rewards competitive personality types while simultaneously trying to consume more resources than it can replenish.

You need to have a well-guarded posture within capitalism. And you'll need to establish boundaries to try to protect your critical resources and replenish them. By design, capitalism-which is built on the ruthless nature of competition-will try to exploit you as a worker.

Under capitalism, you're responsible for protecting yourself.

Protection can come in the form of saying "no" to inappropriate requests, although sometimes power dynamics might not always make that possible. So a more effective alternative may be to say "not right now." Protection can also come in the form of doing your best to set boundaries with your job.

Protecting yourself from exploitation is your own responsibility, unfortunately.

Regardless of the ethics of the company that you work for, you'll always need to be mindful of resource allocation, boundaries, and tactics to try to protect yourself.

Applied Hacking

Technical Bankruptcy (Resource Allocation)

Let's go through an example of resource allocation to examine how an engineering team manages technical debt.

Because the tech industry is competitive, there's often tremendous pressure to ship products as quickly as possible. This pressure to ship products by a given timeline often pushes technical teams to cut corners and introduce unsustainable technical solutions as temporary workarounds to problems. Similar to financial debt, technical debt can often spiral out of control. A single poor decision can lead to future circumstances that further compound the debt. As time progresses, the debt can become overwhelming, and the resources needed to address the debt can exceed the penalties of starting over with a new system.

This threshold where the cost outweighs the reward due to technical debt, is known as *technical bankruptcy*.

Imagine that you're working in an organization and the project that you're assigned to is clearly spiraling into technical bankruptcy. How can you communicate that concern while positioning yourself as effectively as possible in the organization?

This scenario draws on many lessons from this book, including influence, broadcasting, collaboration, and resource allocation.

Recommendation

Your first step is to identify your intended outcome. By now you should already feel that you may be able to influence the situation's many outcomes. But you should figure out what outcome you want before you begin to act.

In this case, let's suppose that you want to scrap the project so that you can replace it with a more sustainable alternative. And in the process, you want to use the migration to the new system as fuel for a raise.

Once you understand the resources needed to sustain that system, you'll need to broadcast your concern. Using influence, you can communicate your concerns about the project to others at the company. The more offensive the technical debt is, the better for your goal. So you need to communicate exactly how much work is required to do a very basic task with the system. If it takes a team of engineers several weeks to do a task that would've otherwise taken a few moments, you need to carefully convey that. And you'll need to show that an alternative will be viable.

Collect data to demonstrate your concerns. This might come in the form of metrics from the engineering team or perhaps the commit logs associated with your work. How you capture the situation doesn't matter—as long as you have the data to back up your messaging.

Focus on collecting data that supports your cause.

As you collect data, you'll begin to see which resources are needed to complete each task. As you identify those resources, you can design a sustainable system that uses fewer resources to do the same thing. As you ultimately address the resource deficit with a new system, you can use this data to support a raise for yourself.

Large companies like Microsoft, Amazon, and Google are fiercely competitive when it comes to compensation among employees. Oftentimes it'll take this level of detail and strong supporting evidence to get the raise that you might be looking for.

And you'll especially need supporting data if you're looking for a raise and you're from a marginalized group. While this sort of double standard is an unfortunate reality, it's at least predictable.

Pressure (Protection)

It can be common to feel a tremendous amount of pressure to perform. Oftentimes that pressure doesn't come from your own desire to compete but rather from your bosses.

> Imagine that you're working at a small tech company, and your boss expects you to dedicate most of your waking hours to the company. You discover that there's almost no way to detach from work because your phone, laptop, and in-office presence keep you coupled to your job. As you begin to exceed the point of sustainability, you start to withdraw from work. Your boss doesn't seem satisfied with your withdrawal, and they begin commenting on the way that your performance is slipping below their inflated expectations. How do you manage the situation so that you don't burn yourself out while keeping your overzealous boss satisfied?

Use resource allocation to frame the situation.

Oftentimes there'll be nuance in a specific working environment, decisions, or focus areas that can be easy to miss at a glance. By design, most leaders won't have a tremendous amount of visibility into specific aspects of work, and so it'll be likely that leaders will be unaware of those nuances.

Using resource allocation and drawing attention to your currency can be an effective way to show that you may be working unsustainably.

Recommendation

I recommend framing the situation as one of exchange.

Point out that you're having to neglect one aspect of your workload in exchange for another. Frame the situation as a choice—or as trade-off between two choices.

For example, you might point out to your boss that you could focus on task A and neglect task B—or you could focus on B and neglect A.

Framing the pressure in this way can help to illustrate to your boss that they'll need to make a choice about which task should take priority over the other.

In this scenario, all the rules of influence, leadership, and collaboration apply. And if there's a task that you'd prefer to focus on, try to influence the decision in your favor. Either way, a decision about which task they'd like you to prioritize should give you the freedom to trade your currency on one for the other.

Spend your currency wisely, and use your currency as a bargaining chip in your favor.

Your time, energy, and currency are finite resources, after all.

Conclusion

Because relationships with the tech industry typically last decades or more, you need to be able to sustain relationships.

You can visualize sustainable tactics in tech by envisioning systems as small factories that need inputs in exchange for outputs.

Work goes in, and money comes out. You can then trade money for a break. Breaks can then support more effective work.

You can observe your systems. You can then capture data about the resources that they need to operate. As you understand the resources, you can make projections about what you need to sustain your systems over time. Given finite resources, it'll quickly become apparent to you whether your systems can replenish themselves quickly enough to continue operating.

The tech industry seems to constantly be trying to take more from us than we can give. This starves and burns out technologists over time. And unless you have a strong mental armor, your career in tech won't be sustainable.

[50] "List of minimum annual leave by country", https://en.wikipedia.org/wiki/List_of_minimum_annual_leave_by_country

Chapter 11. Hacking

You should now have a complete kit of tools, examples, language, and resources to start hacking capitalism.

You should have well-established concepts of the consequences of competition and collaboration in the layers of the tech industry.

You should understand that you can use cooperation to help organizations work together to create stronger products. (Kubernetes is a fantastic example of this type of cooperation in action.)

You should understand that companies in our economy feel that they have absolutely no obligations to the good of society from an ethics perspective. And in my opinion, their lack of ethics shows.

Companies prioritize profits over society and at the expense of society.

I believe that it's safe to say that whatever you're looking for, you know what it is—or that at least you'll know it when you find it.

Personally, my something is reaching a point financially where I can escape from capitalism's hellscape of worker extortion.

I want to buy as much land as possible and give it back to society and to the people. I want to wake up in the morning and—even if for a single day—I want to feel free.

So how do you begin hacking the economy to achieve your goal?

Build Your Workshop

Every hacker needs a computer to do their work.

Every career hacker needs a space where they can work.

The knowledge, relationships, tools, and situations that you surround yourself with will become your workshop.

Naturally, you'll spend some time setting up your environment so that you can be as successful as possible.

For example, if you're working remotely and you're spending most of your time on video calls influencing people, it could be wise to invest into making yourself as comfortable as possible in the process.

You can potentially reinvest your time and energy "profits" back into yourself.

> **Self Investment** is investing your time, energy, and money back into yourself in order to hopefully yield a higher return on investment.

Your workshop is a place where you can invest in yourself. There may be other areas for self-investment such as knowledge, education, access to transportation, and even your proximity to certain people, places, or events.

For example, buying into a social network in Silicon Valley might be a worthwhile choice if networking in Silicon Valley may be an aspect of your career that you had wanted to strengthen.

Buying a car might be a wise investment if you've chosen to put down roots in a city that doesn't have much public-transportation infrastructure.

A productive desk, a reliable internet connection, or even hardware that helps with your work as a technologist are all examples of things you may choose to bring to your workshop.

Ultimately, the best self-investments that I've made in my lifetime have been nonmaterial. The people who I've surrounded myself with, the knowledge I've gained by being around them, and the education that I've given myself have been the only investments that have truly compounded my returns.

The things that make up an effective workshop are unique to each hacker.

Every successful hacker who I know has strong opinions on things like hardware, operating systems, text editors, tools, and so on. But it's also okay if you might not have strong opinions about those sorts of things. As a career hacker, you'll begin developing your own opinions on what tools you chose to wield.

A word of caution to anyone who invests in their workshop: It's possible for you to become too dependent on specific tools. While you can use high-quality tools for efficiency, they should never be something that you can't go without. You need to remain effective even if you don't have access to your usual working environment.

For example, at one point in my life I was working in multiple countries, which meant that I was often showing up for work with minimal or no sleep in strange environments. I didn't always have the luxury of a good night's sleep or a familiar desk. In some situations, even communicating in English wasn't an option.

In these situations, I needed to be able to stay on top of things even without the comfort of my home workshop.

This sentiment also comes into play if you had wanted to get into cybersecurity exploitation. After finding yourself on a foreign machine, it can quickly become apparent that you don't have access to your usual tools, resources, aliases, and shortcuts.

Appreciate your workshop when you have it, but be prepared to work without it.

Select a Target

Whether you're hacking the economy or hacking a computer system, your first steps remain the same: Select your target and then to begin probing for weaknesses.

In penetration testing, you'd do this using network scans: Your goal is to try to understand what options you have that'll respond to you.

In your career, you can do the same by scanning companies for opportunities. Your goal is to identify weaknesses or–at the very least–identify systems that will somehow respond to you.

You'll need to be able to find a target so you can get into the system.

For example, suppose that you want to work at a large tech company such as Google, Tesla, Amazon, or Microsoft.

Your first step is to identify your goal. Most likely your goal isn't actually to get a specific job, but rather the outcome of doing that job.

For example, you probably don't care whether a given production system stays online. What you care about is that you get the paycheck, recognition, and experience that you feel that you deserve for keeping a production system online.

You need to separate your intended outcome (your goal) from how you'll achieve it.

For instance, if by chance you had wanted to live off the land, collecting water and chopping wood could be the way that you'd provide shelter for yourself.

For every goal, there's a set of actions that will get you there.

Intended Outcome	Means of Achievement
Earning $100,000.00 in assets that will keep up with inflation.	A job at a profitable tech corporation such as Google, or Microsoft that pays restricted stock units (RSUs).
Adding a prestigious work item to your resume.	A high ranking job at a well established technical organization in the space.
Buying a home for your family.	A job that is optimized for location and large up front payments.

Connecting your goals to what you want in return can help you stay focused. Naturally, you want to spend your time and energy wisely.

As you figure out what you want from a company, you can begin to map your needs to possible weaknesses or responsive endpoints. If your goal is to earn a certain amount of stock, you need to identify which company is most likely to give you the kind of stock that you're after. Spend time researching your options to narrow them down. And if that might be your goal, you'll also need to gauge which companies' stock prices are more likely to go up.

This is where it can help to draw on collaboration, your network of allies, and a solid hacker crew. With some research, you can derive the types of stock packages that each company gives to employees working at various levels.

Let's say that you conclude that you have a high likelihood of getting hired at a company like Microsoft. And you realize that Microsoft has a history of paying out restricted stock shares to engineers that are similar to the types of assets that you're trying to build.

You now have a decision to make. Is Microsoft where you want to work?

Keep in mind that stock isn't everything.

As I had mentioned, the nonmaterialistic things are the ones that are truly worth investing in. It can oftentimes be more fulfilling in the long run to invest in education, relationships, and knowledge.

Will Microsoft give you access to relationships? Mentorship? Knowledge? Experience?

Maybe a medium-sized company could be a better fit for your needs. Perhaps a job at Microsoft might be out of reach until you gain more experience. Or perhaps Microsoft might just be the wrong fit for you altogether.

Research can be help here.

Given my experience in the tech industry, once I begin to focus on a specific company, my next steps are similar to social engineering. (If you might not be familiar with the term, *social engineering* refers to "the psychological manipulation of people into performing actions or divulging confidential information." [51]) I begin reading articles on Reddit, following leaders on Twitter, researching problems shared from previous employees, and so on.

At some point, you'll decide on a target.

The exact target doesn't matter terribly much. Some, of course, will be easier than others—but in my experience, having a firm target in mind is actually more important than *which* target you have in mind.

So even if you pick the wrong target, that's probably going to be more effective than holding off to try to find the perfect target. You want to start as quickly as possible, so just pick a target to start with. You can always change later.

Penetration Vectors

With a target in mind, you can begin to create leverage by probing for weaknesses.

You can start to probe for weaknesses by looking for a response. In career exploitation, this can be a response to a tweet, a LinkedIn message, or an email.

Your goal here is put together a plan. You want to give yourself some options to choose from by figuring out who you can communicate with.

In hacking the economy, you'll perform a company scan, which will identify the types of product development that seem to be getting attention in a particular organization. You hope to find internal efforts that respond to you.

Your probe might yield an eligible infrastructure department.

Or perhaps the infrastructure department may be missing a senior engineer with deep infrastructure knowledge to mentor other engineers.

Your goal is to figure out exactly where you could fit into the organization or—more importantly—what you could offer the organization.

Understanding competition, collaboration, influence, building, and breaking will all be relevant as you begin your conversations with the organization. I often spend a few moments before an interview and remind myself of their situation. Who are they competing with? How can I demonstrate collaboration? Where will my influence be most effective? How many microeconomies can I infer?

You'll need to be able to collaborate with others in the organization to make yourself valuable. And you need to be able to use influence during the interview. There's an art to identifying an organization's needs from the outside. A lot of it comes from practicing, communicating, networking, and quickly identifying problems.

Mapping noticeable problems in an organization to your skill set can be fruitful. Because there are no shortages of problems in the tech industry. The industry is ruthless, traumatizing, and exploitive. There will be debris everywhere you look, most of which you'll be able to see from the outside.

Learn to celebrate the problems in tech because each problem represents a potential opening that you can exploit.

As you identify problems, the possibilities of being able to insert yourself to solve them begin to illuminate themselves. I often try to look at the industry by identifying an intersection between two things:

- Noticeable problems
- Surplus of money

Where there are problems and money, there are hacking opportunities.

The more problems, the better.

The more money, the better.

The tech industry has both: a lot of problems and a lot of money. Spend time finding the problems that make sense for you, and try to map them to money. The industry is built on competition, which means that the more uncommon your skill set, the more valuable you'll be toward solving a specific problem.

Lateral Movement

In penetration testing, I often need to traverse the network once I've made my first point of contact from the outside.

> **Lateral Movement** is moving horizontally within an organization or context; peer to peer movement.

You can apply the concept of lateral movement to achieving your goals in a company. In other words, getting a job or making a sale is the first half of a two-part strategy. First: get in the door. Next: position yourself for success.

Large companies like Google, Microsoft, and Amazon often have a lifetime of opportunities right inside the same company.

Any given engineer can have many potential futures. They could become a salesperson, then a philanthropist, and ultimately an investor without ever leaving the company. So it can be a strong and viable tactic to get a job in one area and then transition to another area after you've got your foot in the door.

Never underestimate the value of a good transition.

I often remind people who are struggling in their positions or who are burnt out from working on the same concepts day after day that lateral movement can often be a viable option.

As you work to position yourself as effectively as possible with the intent of penetrating inner circles such as the elite, you may find that shifting your position laterally may be worth considering.

A lateral move often comes easily and with low risk, and it can give you valuable insights into other aspects of a company that you'd otherwise be missing.

I've heard CEOs and executives mention that working in as many positions as possible is the best tactic for becoming a well-versed upper-level leader.

Privilege Escalation

In penetration testing, I think of *privilege escalation* as misusing a piece of software or systems paradigm to elevate my privileges at runtime.

> **Privilege Escalation** in hacking capitalism is using tactics such as influence, collaboration, broadcasting, and social engineering to gain access to elevated levels at a tech corporation; breaking into the circles of the elite.

Privilege escalation often means using small pieces of software in ways that they weren't intended for to gain access to other parts of a system. Once you've gained initial access, you can use lateral movement to reach other points of escalation, and so on.

Privilege escalation is also possible within tech organizations.

For example, getting invited to a specific meeting can be the first step in breaching privileged resources such as decision-making.

First, identify the path that you might use and then pursue that path. A lateral move to gain a better position might be viable.

For example, if you know that a weekly meeting is when the engineering team's leaders make decisions during a weekly meeting that will affect your chance for a raise, target that meeting.

Try to understand how others got invited, and try to apply the techniques from this book toward your goal. Once you're inside the meeting, collaborate to influence laterally across the organization. Build trusted relationships with other leaders. Spend the time to build a strong network of trust.

There will be many ways to privilege-escalate beyond your scope of influence in an organization. Collect vectors as often as possible. Listen for them, and home in on ideas on how you can escalate yourself as needed.

And be tactful about when and where you escalate.

Every escalation is ultimately a risk. Every escalation involves spending currency. You'll need to understand the cost of each escalation.

Escalate wisely.

Just because an escalation opportunity may be available, that doesn't always mean that it's worth escalating.

If you're from a marginalized group, your diligence about when you escalate and who you bring with you will have a tremendous effect on your situation.

Oftentimes a single escalation can be the difference between a healthy working environment and the toxic circles of the elite. You'll need to remain supportive, cooperative, and influential if you notice that others are trying to escalate. It can feel natural to think of your colleagues as rivals or competitors when your colleagues escalate toward the elite.

And a single friendly escalation that lifts you in the process can sometimes be as effective as escalating yourself, and it's oftentimes cheaper.

Exiting Cleanly

There's an art to staying undetected during an escalation breach.

If you try to hack capitalism without proper attention to the nuances of doing so, that can often come across as ruthless or cutthroat.

I often liken the tactics in this book to fighting fire with fire. You're merely speaking the language that's available to you. You're using the only tools that seem to have an impact on the situation. What you do with the tools after you've achieved the titles, stature, and money is what can potentially shift the system for the better.

You'll need to maintain a low level of suspicion.

Try not to draw attention to yourself. Because many comfortable members of the elite–without even realizing the consequences of their thoughts–could view your presence not as an equal member who deserves a seat at the table but as a threat.

You'll need to maintain a conservative observable posture to remain undetected and to avoid otherwise being perceived as a threat.

Despite your good intentions, this level of comfort with the system can often be alarming to others. I suggest viewing yourself as if you were an intruder so that you don't let your guard down.

You–the "intruder"–will need to do two things.

- Remain undetected during the breach.
- Remove any identifying information or persistent links.

Basically, you'll need to evade detection and cover your tracks–just like a hacker.

At first this may sound as if I were encouraging you to do something malicious. But these two tactics are practiced throughout the industry, so you won't look out of place doing this.

These are the same tactics that CEOs and startup founders use when they're exiting through a merger or acquisition. Maintain a stable posture, do your work, get paid, and exit cleanly.

You too can use this tactic, and you should follow this pattern if you want to be successful.

> An **exit strategy** is a premeditated plan that targets specific outcomes during a prolonged course of action.

You'll need to give thought to an exit strategy no matter what situation you may be trying to leave.

For example, if you're moving to a leadership position, you'll need to cleanly exit your previous role.

If you're exiting a team, you'll need to make sure that the team isn't left with a substantial void in your absence. It can be risky to try to shift your position in an organization without also shifting your relationships and the surrounding expectations.

Another example of a clean exit strategy is leaving a job on good terms. You'll need to pay special attention to make sure that you maintain a healthy and prosperous working relationship with the company. It can be risky to damage relationships that might be useful later. Don't burn bridges. Remember that under capitalism, companies have only one goal: profit. Those who occupy the system insist on pretending that this isn't the nature of the system. But the sooner that you can understand that this is the case, the safer you'll be.

Which means that for you to be a "good" capitalist, I think that you need to prioritize your own means of profit at all costs. The economy is built on competition, after all. Use the competition to your advantage.

You have to look out for yourself if you want to survive in this system.

I often remind myself of a few takeaways that I've learned in my years in the tech industry.

For example, your relationship with an organization is only as good as the monetary gains that come with it. Nothing more. Nothing less. As long as you're making money and you're on board with the type of work that you're doing, the relationship is worth maintaining. The moment you're no longer achieving your goals, the relationship becomes counterproductive.

The tech industry isn't your family.

Your job is a vehicle to a paycheck. Your paycheck is a vehicle to your dreams.

If you don't continuously grow closer to your goals, the tech industry will exploit you until there's nothing left. Leaving one company for another can be a viable path, especially for people from marginalized groups who've hit a glass ceiling.

To be extremely direct about it, if you're from a marginalized group, there's little chance that you'll find a reciprocal relationship with a single company. So you'll likely put in more into a job than you'll get back. The best thing to do in this situation is to leverage the fact that capitalism is built on competition: Begin having conversations with anyone willing to pay you what you're worth.

I can't stress this enough: Leaving a company may in most cases be the correct choice. Especially if you're from a marginalized group or you're overworked or you're underappreciated. Unfortunately, given the state of the tech industry, that's most likely the case.

There may be other reasons for leaving a company. Money, stock, and title have little meaning if you're unhappy and dissatisfied with the person who you've become.

Personally, I've walked away from a sizable amount of stock because the corporation's ethics didn't align with my values.

At the time, this misalignment hurt me, but in hindsight, I'm now of a mind that the company has no obligation to society. It was my fault for believing that a company would ultimately choose to accommodate experiences like mine over their profits.

In hindsight, I should've been able to predict their negligence.

Whatever your reason for leaving a company, perhaps the most straightforward tactic is that you should be honest about your situation: If you could get paid more elsewhere, it's in your best interest to leave. Full stop.

If you can't get an equitable relationship from a company-or even a reasonable but imbalanced relationship-it's in your best interest to leave. Especially if you can find what you're looking for elsewhere.

Compounding Hacks

Performing a single hack involves selecting a target, exploiting the target, achieving a goal, and exiting cleanly.

This can come in the form of getting a job with a company or gaining a position of influence in an open-source project. This might also come in the form of gaining a business-to-business sales relationship or a consulting contract.

No matter what form a hack might come in, you'll need to be able to link the hacks together.

Your relationships will likely span many instances of a single hack. And your relationships will help you move on to bigger and more impressive hacks.

For example, I've worked closely with colleagues who've ended up later becoming managers of mine. In other situations, close relationships have become customers or partners of mine. As my career have grown, investment opportunities have presented themselves.

I eventually discovered that my relationships were worth more to me than any single job.

Don't ever end a relationship unless you're sure that it's the right time to end. Otherwise, a temporary pause or a break is often the best approach.

Regardless of your relationships, a single hacked environment can be useful for hacking future environments.

You'll need to apply this approach to your career.

Get your foot in the door with a large company, and make as many connections as possible. Use your relationships and your knowledge to further your initiatives. Use one hack to reinforce future work.

There's a fine line between using social engineering and being a skilled and productive capitalist.

Personally, I draw the line at intents and outcomes. As long as your intention isn't to hurt anyone or to damage a company, I believe that a fair amount of networking is appropriate.

Keep in mind that I'm in no way encouraging you to harm or damage any company. In fact, I'm encouraging just the opposite.

Be resourceful and take full advantage of the many opportunities made available to you. Lift others up as you work toward your goals.

Be honest about your goals and your intentions. There's nothing wrong with wanting a brighter future for yourself and your colleagues.

Be realistic about the amount of effort that people from marginalized groups need to expend to succeed under capitalism. That said, not everyone may be ready to acknowledge the absurd amount of detail and work that people from marginalized groups have to put in to get to the same levels as their competitors in tech.

Conclusion

Hacking capitalism takes work and dedication. As it turns out, access to knowledge and expectation setting seems to be the most difficult aspect of the solving the puzzle.

There's a good chance that hacking capitalism will offend people and repulse those who aren't prepared to see the amount of work that it takes to achieve economic parity with those who were born into privilege.

Hacking capitalism will likely repulse those who don't see the broader system in play.

Even if you hack capitalism for good reasons or otherwise positively affect your life or your environment, you'll inevitably use deliberate tactics to predict behaviors and further your self-interest.

These truths can be hard for many privileged people to reconcile. Not everyone is ready to admit to themselves that the economy is a zero-sum game, especially in tech.

Privileged workers in the tech industry aren't all prepared to compete with this level of tactful direction. But this level of hypercompetition should come as no surprise to you.

Many technologists-including those who are straight, white, or male-come from a place of privilege where existing in the economy is easier for them. To them, the thought of people from marginalized groups having to overwork themselves and leverage advanced strategies to get promoted might feel like an unfair amount of work. And that's because it is an unfair amount of work.

Of course, there's no guarantee that any of my tactics will work.

Using these tactics also brings with them an increased risk for people from marginalized groups.

But having these basic rules, systems, and expectations can dramatically prepare you for the onslaught of trauma in tech.

Remember that competition is the antisystem to collaboration. Competition within companies evolves into hypercompetition, and it eventually breaks. Collaboration ensues and the cycle repeats.

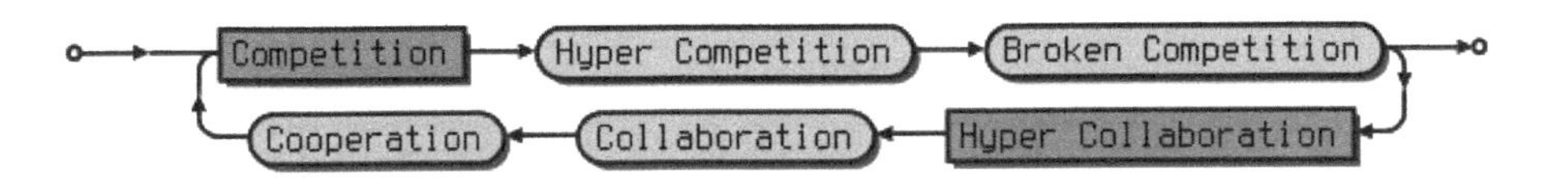

These elements of human behavior come in waves. Teams will resort to tribalism during traumatic waves, and they'll begin competing with other teams in an organization.

On the other hand, during moments of tranquility, teams may begin to collaborate and form unions in cooperation. Try to identify these behaviors, and try to predict when they'll shift.

Connect your actions to your goals, and keep your goals front of mind.

I think that understanding culture and influence will be most of your day job, outside of your normal day-job responsibilities. The ability to craft software is just one part of the work that you do each day.

Part of advocating for yourself in the tech industry is prioritizing your needs in your career. This is especially true if you're from a marginalized group.

I'm drawing attention to the extreme ruthlessness that the tech industry imposes on those who are in it. I actively encourage you to match this level of ruthlessness as you pursue your hopes and dreams.

If there's one thing to take away from this book, it's the importance of being realistic about your situation. Research, education, and accurate expectations for yourself can help to uncover the hidden truths behind the systems that both hurt us and help us.

I want to encourage you to be prepared for the tech industry.

The tech industry can be ruthlessly competitive, and decidedly unfair especially for a marginalized person. However, the tech industry can also offer some of the most wonderful economic advantages to those that occupy it.

I want you to feel equipped and empowered to fight your way toward the elite in any situation. I want you to understand your options and to understand which of them will be effective toward fighting for what you're after.

I also hope that those that read the book one day become a new generation of elite which bring more empathy and compassion for the marginalized communities that may exist in tech. It is all of our responsibility to keep the industry moving forward.

My hope is that you use these skills and tools to build a great tomorrow where technology is equally exciting but substantially less harmful—and where hacking capitalism is no longer needed to survive.

Thought I'd have something more to say.

[51] Wikipedia, s.v. "Social engineering (security)," last modified June 30, 2022, 10:30, https://en.wikipedia.org/wiki/Social_engineering_(security).

Appendix

Ashley Bischoff

Ashley Bischoff, the editor of Hacking Capitalism, is a copy editor based in Dallas. She has a knack for taming technical and business writing, and she's a heartfelt advocate for plain language. Ashley is also a longtime supporter of workers' rights, and she firmly believes that all workers deserve a union.

If you might be interested in unionizing your workplace, an organization such as @CODE_CWA-the group working with labor organizers at places like Activision Blizzard, Google, and NPR-can help you get the ball rolling. Outside of work, Ashley enjoys drinking tea, skating, and kicking back to tracks from In Flames and Lorna Shore. And if you're looking to work with a copy editor, you can tweet her at @FriendlyAshley or contact her at FriendlyEditing.com.

Erratum

If you have discovered any discrepancies, print errors, typos, or have any qualms with the text you can leverage my public erratum resource located on GitHub. New versions of the text will be released as changes are reconciled.

- https://github.com/kris-nova/erratum

Twitch

An extremely special section dedicated to everyone who has supported me writing this absolutely ridiculous book.

This book wouldn't be possible without the countless Twitch supporters who watched me write the pages of this book live.

Definitions

Many of the definitions used in this book are modified version of definitions found in © 2022 Merriam-Webster dictionary, Oxford University dictionary copyright © 2022 Oxford University Press, and Oxford languages Copyright © 2022 Oxford University Press. All rights reserved.

At times, the definitions were modified to illustrate the intended message of the book.

A Note on High and Low Context Communication

Erratum was suggested by @zjreid1 on GitHub [52] to clarify the source and meaning of the definitions offered in this book.

The discrepancy arises in how the communication is referenced, and how the context is **assumed**.

For example if an individual assumes their audience has a high-level of context, they may speak briefly. Whereas the context that is assumed is high, the context that is **offered** is now low.

Several references were provided in reference of "high-context culture" and "low-context culture". [53] [54] [55]

The original definitions found in the book were left in their original form, however this additional reference has been added to the appendix to clarify the difference in how the language can be described.

Release Notes

v0.0.1 Initial. For pre-release.

v0.0.2 Discovered my Bitcoin opinion had been reversed in editing. Updated opinion, and added morality definition.

v0.0.3 Typos and formatting.

v0.0.4 Typos and formatting. Credit (@GANit_ak). Boilerplate metaphor improvements. Credit (@oxinabox).

v0.1.0 Margin update for print. Moving the entire page center to the left 0.10 in. Ready for global.

v0.1.2 Removed leftover icon "fas " references inline.

v0.1.3 Fixed errata. Credit (@ylm). Expanded broadcasting section to include starting small. Embedding a better .pdf for the cover image in the release artifacts on GitHub.

v0.1.4 More errata. Fixed versioning inline. Thanks to @zjreid1 and @ylm for thier contributions to the work.

v0.1.5 Typos from Amazon KDP. Epub finally added to the manuscript!

v0.1.6 Typos from Erratum. Thanks to @fabianhjr (github) @trolldere (discord) and @WarpSpeed17 (twitter)

[52] Low vs. High Context Communication, https://github.com/kris-nova/erratum/issues/5

[53] https://open.maricopa.edu/com110/chapter/1-5-cultural-characteristics-and-communication/

[54] https://www2.pacific.edu/sis/culture/pub/context_cultures_high_and_lo.htm

[55] https://www.state.gov/courses/answeringdifficultquestions/html/app.htm?p=module3_p3.htm